A rural gathering for an opera

A crowd watching the opera at the renowned Norbulingka Park in Lhasa, Tibet Autonomous Region

A niche containing the statue of the God of Tibetan Opera

Meeting the audience

Young actors and actresses at rehearsal

A scene from a Tibetan opera performed at the Norbulingka Park during the Shoton Festival in Lhasa

Stage props in Tibetan opera:

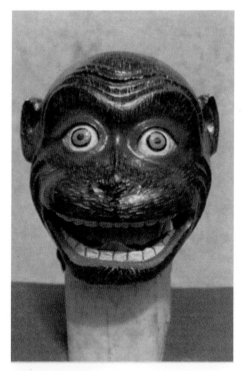

Mask of a monkey

A demon's mask

The costume of horse

Mask of a divine being

A hunter's mask

A wedding costume

Costumes for elderly men and women

A dance scene in Tibetan opera

Statues of Srongb-tsan Sgam-po, King of Tibet, (left) and Princess Wencheng, enshrined in the Potala Palace, Lhasa, Tibet Autonomous Region

Princess Wencheng received by King Srongb-tsan Sgam-po upon her arrival
in Lhasa in "Princess Wencheng"

The title character of "Maiden Snang-sa"

Grags-pa-bsam-grub, Snang-sa's husband

Chieftain Grags-chen-pa's trusted attendant

Pad-ma-vod-vbar's parents in "Pad-ma-vod-vbar"

One of the dragon girls in "Pad-ma-vod-vbar"

A scene showing the God of Longevity

A ferryboat

Heavenly fairies

TALES FROM TIBETAN OPERA

Edited by Wang Yao

NEW WORLD PRESS

Second Edition 2013

Edited by Wang Yao

Translated by Wang Yao

Cover Design by He Yuting

Copyright by **New World Press**, Beijing, China

ISBN 978-7-5104-4104-2

Published by

NEW WORLD PRESS

24 Baiwanzhuang Street, Beijing 100037, China

Distributed by

NEW WORLD PRESS

24 Baiwanzhuang Street, Beijing 100037, China

Tel: 86-10-68995968

Fax: 86-10-68998705

Website: www.newworld-press.com

E-mail: frank@nwp.com.cn

Printed in the People's Republic of China

Preface to the Second Edition

This is an old work of mine completed more than 20 years ago. It was sold out soon after it was published by the New World Press and, for the time being, can hardly be found on the market. Now, having won the approval from the competent publishing authorities, I have made the decision to have it reprinted, and I would like to take this opportunity to speak my mind:

1. This book, having suffered from numerous criticisms during the Cultural Revolution, almost went into extinction. Indubitably, I myself went through harsh criticism and accusation, most of which were, as it turned out, utterly false. Luckily, all this is gone. Now that everything has developed along the right lines, we might just as well let that pass.

2. Currently, Tibetan opera has become a striking symbol of the cultural development on the Chinese mainland and a dazzlingly beautiful flower in the blossoming garden of Chinese opera, which is, in essence, the fruit of the unremitting efforts of Tibetan writers and actors. Apart from the innovations in form, aria, masks, costume, music, etc, the plots of Tibetan opera themselves are marvelous spectacles with salient national traits which have won great popularity among the Chinese people. In view of this, I, as a promoter and translator of Tibetan opera, feel fairly gratified. Never shall we forget that since the 13th century, writers of successive dynasties have spared no efforts in adapting stories of the Buddhist scriptures to Tibetan opera. Thanks to their originality and superb artistic taste, unique aria and dance have been formed to express the fairly complex emotions

of the characters of the opera which strike a sentimental chord in the audience, hence a complete pattern of Tibetan opera taking shape.

Undergoing vigorous development and promotion, Tibetan opera, one of the important inheritors of Tibetan culture, has played a crucial role in carrying forward our national culture. Thanks to the performances of Tibetan opera touring the rural and urban areas of Tibet and its continuous development, it has become more and more popular throughout China. What is to be introduced here is just the stories about the eight major Tibetan operas, and new repertoires remain to be collected and brought forth.

Also, the forms of Tibetan opera have witnessed tremendous changes. To be more exact, performances are staged in theaters rather than on squares; previously, the audience was just composed of farmers and herdsmen. Now, almost all rural and urban residents have become Tibetan opera fans. Moreover, music and costumes in the opera have been greatly improved. Getting close to the actual conditions, daily life and the common people has become the new developmental orientation of Tibetan opera. To develop a strong socialist culture in China, it is critical to inspire the cultural creativity of the whole nation. On the part of myself, I think Tibetan opera has a promising future. In this sense, the reprinting of this book *Tales from Tibetan Opera* serves to be a small gift of mine.

Recently, Mr. Tsering Namgyal, a teacher from the University of Tibet, paid a visit to me. He has been working for his doctorate in the Tibetan opera program in the Central Conservatory of Music, which further shows that Tibetan opera has won its due attention in the research field.

Preface

The English edition of *Tales from Tibetan Opera* presented here is a collection of eight Tibetan stories frequently performed in Tibet.

The book is a first attempt to give the reader a thorough explanation of the main performance content of Tibetan opera. Previously the only studies available in French and English were the French Tibetologist Professor J. Bacot's introduction to three stories of Tibetan opera, and Professor T. Norbu's account of one Tibetan opera. Their work has undoubtedly been of great help to later studies. As for my contribution to Tibetan studies, I can only quote a Tibetan proverb, "What I know is only a drop in the oceans of knowledge."

I hope this book will be of help to the reader, especially to those interested in the magnificent natural scenery of the Tibetan pastures, and in the simple life, religious beliefs and unique customs of the Tibetan people. In addition, it will help the reader gain an understanding of the artistic creativity and taste of the people and understand how the study of Tibetan opera can be enjoyable and interesting.

I am deeply grateful to Dr. Barbara N. Aziz for inviting me to attend the Third International Seminar on Tibetology, sponsored by Columbia University of New York in the summer of 1982. It was Dr. Aziz who gave me the opportunity to present my thesis, *Tibetan Opera and Tales from Tibetan Opera*. The warm reception and extensive interest of colleagues attending the meeting spurred me to write this English edition. Dr. Aziz also discussed the manuscript with me in person, for which I offer my thanks.

3

Mrs. Ouyang Caiwei, though in her 70s, extended meticulous and constructive help with the English translation of the book. Such generosity was indeed overwhelming.

Additionally, Professor Ernst Steinkellner, president of the Faculty of Tibetology and Buddhology of Vienna University, did the revision of the manuscript while I was a visiting professor there from 1982 to 1983. He put forward perceptive suggestions on the entire book and improved its English.

Last but not least I would like to thank Mr. Sna-kha-rtse-blo-bzang-rdo-rje, my old friend and colleague. It would have been impossible to bring this book into being without his kind assistance. His profound and erudite knowledge of Tibetan opera and performing art and his rich experience in directing opera have been indispensable to this project.

I welcome readers' opinions and of course remain responsible for any errors in this book.

The principles of writing the Tibetan language followed in this book are as follows:

ka, kha, ga, nga/ca, cha, ja, nya/

ta, tha, da, ha/ pa, pha, ba, ma/

tsa, tsha, dza, wa/ zha, za, va, ya/

fa, la, sha, sa/ha, a/ i, u, e, o.

Contents

TIBETAN OPERA AND TALES
FROM TIBETAN OPERA

by Wang Yao

I

Tibetan opera is a comprehensive performing art which presents stories through the media of singing and dancing. It is prevalent not only in Tibet but in Sichuan, Yunnan, Gansu and Qinghai provinces. Wherever there are large communities of Tibetans, it is popular.

In the Tibetan language, opera is called A-lce-lhamo, the actor lha-mo-ba and the script khrab-gzhung.

Tibetan opera is one of the oldest drama forms among the people of Central Asia. Artists, playwrights and others believe that opera was introduced by Thang-stong-rgyal-po, a monk of the Bkav-rgyud Sect (the White Sect) of Tibetan Buddhism, whose religious teachings were handed down orally from generation to generation. As the playwright of the opera "Prince Spring-gzhon" said in its preface: "In the old days, Vphrin-las-rje-btsun, called Thang-stong rgyal-po, who had a good command of the principles of life, was the most accomplished person in our snowy land. His Holiness Vphrin-las used performances to educate the people. He spread marvelous songs and dances like a canopy over the people of all tribes and influenced their minds with holy religious teachings and biographies of great men. Hence, the

1

Tibetan opera, superb in skills, rites and systems, emerged."* This opinion is rather widespread.

According to the book *Chronological Table of Great Events of Orthodox White Gem*,** Thang-stong-rgyal-po was born in the year of the Female Wood Ox in the sixth cycle of sixty years in the Tibetan calendar (1385 A.D.). In accordance with the above-mentioned opinion, Tibetan opera originated between the fourteenth and fifteenth centuries. But, judging by the records of the earlier period, it was first only pantomime with an emphasis on dancing.*** Only after absorbing and building literary content did it become a performing art that focused on acting and singing. Evidence from surviving murals and historical records shows that at the latest, in the period of Ngagdbang-blo-bzang-rgya-mtsho, the fifth Dalai Lama (1617-1682), Tibetan opera had developed into the kind of performance seen today.

The text, dance, melodies, masks and costumes of Tibetan opera seem to have gradually taken shape by assimilating some religious

---

* In the collection of the Central Institute of Nationalities.

** Written by Sangs-rgyas rgya-mtsho in the seventeenth century, in the collection of the Central Institute of Nationalities.

*** There was a lost theatrical item entitled "Dpav-Vkhum" in Sa-skya, in western Tibet. According to artist Dbang-rgyal's narration, it was pantomime that stressed dancing. In addition, the book *Sa-skya Gynealogy* contained the following record: "Vkhon, Treasure-king, was born in the Male Wood Dog year of the Tibetan calendar (1034 A.D.). In his early days he listened to and became well-acquainted with the teachings of his father and elder brother. He admired new and old Tantra (Buddhist religious writings that are mystical in nature). He attended a large temple fair in Vbro, which was held at that time. Among acrobatics and other theatrical shows, many sorcerers and twenty-eight women who had a good command of the principles of life put on masks and carried weapons and presented diverse dances, to the accompaniment of the beating of drums by women with long queues. Really splendid! All this illustrates that it was in the stage of pantomime.

rites exorcising evil spirits and propitiating the gods, and episodes from folk tales and Buddhist Sutras, based on Tibetan folk dances, songs, ballad-singing and story narration. In the course of its development, countless artists, playwrights and other groups of people, as well as drama lovers in the upper social strata, constantly refined and enriched its form. As a result, it evolved into the Tibetan opera of today, richly colored with the style and distinctive characteristics of its own nationality.*

In the old days, Tibetan opera was mainly performed in public squares except for the area of Bla-brang (Xiahe) in southern Gansu Province, where the performances were presented on stages due to the influence of Han** operatic forms. The actors used simple make-up and masks so the audience could distinguish whether the characters were good, bad, loyal or vicious from the shape and color of the masks. Narrators told the audience the plots of the operas in short ballads.

When the actors came on stage, they danced to the rhythm of percussion instruments. While an actor sang, other actors behind the stage sang in chorus. As the performances were in public squares outdoors, the actors sang in high, resonant, powerful voices, and the melodies vibrated in the robust style of the highland people. This tradition continues today in indoor performances.

At least twenty melodies have been found in scripts read by the author. They expressed the ideas and feelings of men, women, old and

---

* Shown in the murals of the Potala Palace and on page 95 in the book *History of Kings and Ministers in Tibet* (dpyid-kyi-rgyal-movi-glu-dbyangs in the edition of the Nationalities Publishing House).

** China's majority nationality, which makes up over 93 percent of China's total population.

young: joy, sorrow, grief and ecstasy. The following table shows four of them:

Melody	Mood presented in operas
gdang-ring	joy, ease of mind
skyo-glu	sorrow, grief
gdang-thung	narration in general
gdang-log	emotional change, undulating moods

During performances, actors often changed the melodies, varying them with the development of the plot, which subtly expressed the emotions of the characters and portrayed the thoughts deep in their hearts. For instance, in "Maiden Snang-sa," the heroine uses several different melodies to express changes in her surroundings and diverse moods. In the opera "Prince Nor-bzang," the melody sung in his going-out-to-battle differs from that sung on his return to the palace.

Dancing movements in Tibetan opera go well with the lyrics and melodies and are linked to the development of the plot. In general, they are drawn from movements in everyday life but are refined and exaggerated, giving the audience an aesthetic sense of harmony and vigor. Some movements, such as bowing with hands clasped, and salutation, show traces of the religious rites of the early period. The dancing movements may be classified into the following six types according to postures and rhythms:

Name of dance	Style	Content presented
don-vdar	from slow to quick tempo; moving up and down	on entering the stage
phye-ling	turning in half circles, first to the right, then to the left	in marching forward
phyag-vbul	raising hand to salute, bowing with hands clasped	in salutation
gar-che	turning in whole circles; moving in a ring	treading on a long journey
dal-gtong	slow steps	with all musical instruments at a standstill for an intermission
vphar-chen	turning large circles, spinning with arms extended at an angle of 60 degrees to the ground	martial skills; acrobatics

Except for presentations of selected extracts from full-length operas, Tibetan opera is divided into three parts in performances.

First part: *Don or rngon-pa don*. It serves as a prologue to the performance, introducing all actors to the audience; performing some songs, dances and comical acts designed to draw in the audience and prepare for the performance of the opera.

Second part: The main body of the opera, the *gzhung*.

Third part: *Btera-shis*, or the epilogue. It refers to the rite for blessing or good augury at the end of the opera. Actors also render songs and dances while accepting donations from the audience.

Performances of Tibetan opera in Tibet begin during the Zhol-ston Festival in the seventh and eighth months of the Tibetan calendar, an annual Tibetan opera festival held in Nor-bu-gling-kha, Lhasa. Theatrical troupes gather in Lhasa to give performances and then go on a performance tour. Amateur theatrical troupes also start their performances during this period.

In the feudal society of serfdom, the actors of the Tibetan opera led as miserable a life as other serfs. Apart from the usual corvee, or duty, they were also burdened with a "performance corvee." Even the Tibetan opera performances at the Zhol-ston Festival were also a sort of U-lag (corvee). But they (actors and actresses) eked out their livelihood on scanty donations and by farming a small plot of land which the manorial lords rented to them. They had to give the lords a part or even the whole of their crop and do corvee labor for them whenever ordered to do so. They were menaced by starvation and diseases and suffered humiliation from officials and aristocrats. This seriously affected the development of opera and the improvement of its artistry. Many opera troupes declined, but thanks to the consistent efforts of a few actors who remained faithful to theatrical art in precarious times, this precious artistic heritage survived.

The artists did not make their painstaking efforts in vain. Since the 1950s, Tibetan opera has bloomed with a new vitality. Owing to the attention of the artists and the people, a state-owned Tibetan opera troupe was formed in Tibet. Bkra-shis-don-grub (who died in 1965) and other famous artists became leaders of theatrical troupes. Privately owned and amateur theatrical troupes have also made vigorous progress.

Actors have been respected more than ever before. Bkra-shis-don-grub attended the Third National Congress of Writers and Artists and was elected a standing committee member of the All-China Federation of the Literary and Art Circles in 1960. Many veteran actors have been elected members of the local political consultative conferences and deputies to the local people's congresses and have taken an active part in the political activities of the country. A number of pieces chosen from the Tibetan opera for the program of national theatrical festivals have been popular among the people of China's various groups, very different from the days before 1949. As Bkra-shis-don-grub said, "Spring comes to the withered tree and flowers blossom again."

Guided by the principle in literature and art of "letting a hundred flowers blossom and weeding the old to bring forth the new," writers and artists have studied and rearranged the traditional features of Tibetan opera. They have improved costumes, stage props, settings and make-up by assimilating elements of the classical operas of the Han culture. Just as Tibetan opera has been influenced by the Han operas, its traditions have affected operatic forms and stories in the provinces of Sichuan, Gansu and Qinghai. And in the past, Chinese operatic art has also had an effect on Japanese, Korean and Vietnamese operas, while itself borrowing from certain Indian traditions.

With social progress and the development of production in Tibet, economic prosperity and cultural efflorescence will inevitably affect Tibetan opera, which reflects social life and is bound to respond to the new cultural development in Tibet.

II

To appreciate the legacy and study the history of Tibetan opera, it is necessary to delve into the stories of the operas. They are mostly drawn from folk tales, history, legends, Buddhist scriptures and social customs.

The famous opera "Princess Wencheng" is a representative piece with a historical theme. Princess Wencheng, Srongb-tsan Sgam-po and Blon-ston-btsan were heroic personages who had great influence in history. Princess Wencheng's arrival in Tibet played a great role in the material and cultural development of Tibetan society. The playwright wrote an opera about her marriage to Srongb-tsan Sgam-po, for performance, portraying the people's praises of the couple, who mirror their own aspirations and feelings. Even today, we find verses in praise of Princess Wencheng among the folk songs, for example:

On the fifteenth day of the lunar calendar,
Princess Wencheng promises to come to Tibet,
Be not afraid of the vast Lotus Flatland,
One hundred fine horses will come to welcome you;
Be not afraid of mountain peaks towering into clouds,
One hundred ox-yak offspring will come to welcome you;
Be not afraid of broad and rapid river currents,
One hundred cattle-hide rafts will come to welcome you.[*]

People's esteem and admiration for Princess Wencheng were mentioned more than once in historical records. For instance, "Records on Tubo" (today's Tibet) in the *New Annals of Tang Dynasty* (618-907) reports:

Srongb-tsan Sgam-po, king of Tibet, sent minister Blon-ston-btsan as an envoy to the capital to pay a tribute of five

_____

[*] *Folk Rhymes of Tibet*, Tibetan edition, p.111.

thousand taels of gold and other highly valued treasures as gifts for betrothal. In 641, the Emperor gave Princess Wencheng of the royal house in marriage to King Srongb-tsan Sgam-po. He issued an imperial edict to appoint the Prince of Jiangxia, Li Daozong, to escort the Princess to Tibet with an imperial scepter. The Prince built a hostel in the kingdom of the Prince of Heyuan.

Srongb-tsan Sgam-po led troops to Bohai, the White Lake, to welcome the Princess. He greeted Li Daozong respectfully, observing the proprieties of a son-in-law. He felt timid and bashful at the sight of the splendid Chinese costumes and ornaments. When he returned to Tibet, he reflected that no king in Tibet had ever married the daughter of an emperor, so he built a citadel and a palace for the princess as a demonstration for later generations....

He sent brothers and sons of nobles to the Imperial Academy to study the *Book of Songs* and the *Book of History*. He requested scholars to annotate books and translate them into the Tibetan language. He also requested silkworm seeds, wine brewers, grain millers and other artisans. An imperial edict confirmed all these requests....

Srongb-tsan came to pay tribute at the Chinese court. He replied with wit and intelligence to the Emperor's questions. Satisfied, Emperor Taizong promoted him to be Right Senior General.

In addition, the *History of Royal Lineage in Tibet*, a book completed in 1388 by Tibetan scholar Bsod-nams-rgyal-mtshan, an abbot of the Sa-skya Sect, contains the following record:

Minister Mgar again came to the King's presence, asking his

permission to make the journey to welcome the Chinese princess to Tibet. Emperor Taizong promised to marry the Princess to the Tibetan King. The Princess requested that she be bestowed a statue of Shakya (the Guardian) and a hoard of treasure as her dowry, and the Emperor complied with her request. So the Princess and her women attendants went to Tibetan minister Mgar, saying: "Minister, a statue of Shakya and countless treasures will be brought to your kingdom. Is there soil in your kingdom suitable for planting trees and vegetables? Are there pebbles? Are there mulberry trees, lilies and turnips?"

Mgar replied: "We have everything you have just mentioned except turnips." Hence, turnip seeds were brought. Then a sedan chair was made and a statue of Sakyamuni was placed in it, carried by two strongmen of the Han nationality named Kyala-ko and Lu-ka. Also, many horses, mules and camels were sent to transport jewelry, silks, satins, clothes, ornaments and other objects necessary for the journey. A banquet was given in honor of the Tibetan minister. The Princess was dressed in a costume decorated with pearls and gems. She and her twenty-five beautiful women attendants rode on horseback. Her parents and ministers escorted her for a short distance.*

The opera "Princess Wencheng" is drawn from such historical data and folk legend, enriched with artistic imagination, and has become widely loved. In the course of building up their common motherland, the Hans and the Tibetans developed flesh-and-blood ties and profound

---

* *History of Royal Lineage in Tibet* (Rgyal-rabs-gsal-bavime-long), Commercial Press, p. 38.

friendship sprang up. Srongb-tsan Sgam-po, Princess Wencheng and Blon-ston-btsan, as depicted in the opera, reflect the encouragement of kinship and unity between the two peoples. Although history books and folk rhymes also praise these characters, the opera presents this theme in a symbolic way and shows the ideal as a social base for daily life.

In the opera, in order to win Princess Wencheng's hand for the Tibetan king, Blon-ston-btsan had to win many contests, such as the five challenges put to the envoys who came to ask for the hand of the Princess for their rulers. He succeeded in putting a silk thread through a zigzag pearl, drinking many cups of wine without getting drunk, getting a hundred colts to identify their mares, and identifying the Princess among three hundred beautiful ladies on the parade ground. His success in the contests shows his folk skills, intelligence and down-to-earth wisdom. As such, the laboring people identify with him in their aspirations and imagination.

A fairytale world appears in the operas, it reflects how the Tibetans cherish the landscape on the highlands. It is worthwhile to prize such feelings of rustic simplicity. Such operas, based on historical legends, bring into prominence what should be stressed and discard what should be left out. This shows the superb skill of the playwrights and artists. They neither deviated from historical reality nor were confined to historical data. They were faithful to the historical facts while giving necessary artistic refinement, so the operas have clear-cut themes and vivid characterizations.

"Prince Nor-bzang" can be considered a representative opera based on a folktale. It is a mythological opera portraying love between a man and a goddess. The story first appeared in a collection of ancient stories, "Fabulous Tree Capable of Responding to Every Wish" (date of its completion unknown). It was entitled "Romance of Nor-bzang" and recorded as a Tibetan opera in the book *History of Kings and Ministers in Tibet** which appeared in the seventeenth century. *Love Song of Tshangs-dbyangs-rgya-mtsho,*** a book which came out a short time afterward, is also a love song with this story as a metaphor. The preface of the opera in manuscript form says: "The writer Tshe-ringd-bang-rgyal saw that 'Song of Nor-bzang' was restricted by ancient lyrics and rules of rhyming and had some defects in performance. So, he adapted it into the opera 'Prince Nor-bzang.' "*** The synopsis follows:

Prince Nor-bzang of the northern kingdom, Pangsldan-pa, was wise, handsome and very popular. In his kingdom was a hunter named Spangs-legs-byin-pa who had saved the dragon king from danger and received magical ropes with which he caught the goddess Yidvphrog-lha-mo. Guided by a hermit in the mountain, the hunter offered her to Prince Nor-bzang, who married her.

Nor-bzang and Yid-vphrog got on well together and were an affectionate couple. But the prince's concubines were jealous of Yid-vphrog-lha-mo and colluded with the court sorcerer, scheming to make the king force Prince Nor-bzang to fight in a distant place so they could then murder Yid-vphrog. The goddess escaped and,

---

* This is a collection of ancient stories, and the date of its completion is unknown.

** From page 102 of the book "Love Song of Tshangs-dbyangs-rgya-mtsho" (compiled by Prof. Yu Daoquan and with the Appendix of Chinese and English translations, and sounds noted down by Prof. Zhao Yuanren), the Fifth of a Series, published by the Institute of History and Languages of the National Central Research Academy, SINICA.

*** This is the work of Ngag-dbang-blo-bzang-gya-mtsho, the Fifth Dalai Lama. The opera was mentioned elsewhere in this book under the title of "Story of Yid-vphrog-ma" but, as a matter of fact, it was another name of the opera.

helped by the queen, flew back to the palace of heaven. When Prince Nor-bzang returned from war to the palace and saw that his beloved had departed, he was filled with grief and anger. Surmounting every difficulty and undergoing all sorts of hardship, he went to the palace of heaven and met Yid-vphrog, welcoming the goddess back to the world, where they lived happily ever after.

Tibetan opera has a strong flavor of folk myth and retains the romanticism of creative folk writing. As Karl Marx said in his introduction to *A Contribution to the Critique of Political Economy*: "Greek mythology is not only the arsenal of Greek art but also its foundation," we can say that Tibetan mythology is the foundation of Tibetan opera.

The opera "Prince Nor-bzang" does not depict the affairs of everyday life but those of goddesses, princes, hermits, deities and supernatural beings, and some phenomena in everyday life. Maxim Gorky described mythology as "the reflection of natural phenomena, the fight against nature and artistic generalization of social life."[*]

"Prince Nor-bzang" portrays man's pride and confidence in conquering nature. Man can catch and marry a goddess who lingers during the life of the world. In short, the opera sings praises of man's power—does this not reflect ancient people's yearning to conquer nature? The operas "Goddess of Marriage" and "Scholar Zhang Boils the Sea at Shamen Island" are of the same tone.

The opera praises faithful love. Indeed, it shows how irrational the old system of marriage was. People can breathe in true love and pure, lofty feelings. For example, Prince Nor-bzang resists the orders of his father, the king, ignores the high status of a king, looks down upon the temptations of beautiful women and passionately loves Yid-vphrog-

---

* *Soviet Literature*, the New Literature and Art edition, p. 2.

lha-mo at all times. Finally, those who are truly in love become husband and wife for good. Such ideas were of progressive significance in a feudal society of serfdom.

A number of folk tales portray the struggle between good and evil, truth and the demon. They have been absorbed into Tibetan opera and adapted into some pieces. "Gzugs-kyi-nyi-ma" is one such piece. In this opera, kind-hearted, gentle and beautiful Gzugs-kyi-nyi-ma stands on the side of truth but is persecuted by her enemy, who represents evil, ferocity and ugliness. She undergoes suffering and tortures just like the kind-hearted and industrious laboring people who were oppressed, exploited and humiliated in real life of that period. But final victory is always on the side of truth. People cannot cope with irrational phenomena in their complicated everyday life; they have to express their needs and aspirations through imagination.

It appears it was at a rather late date that playwrights searched for material for their operas among social customs. The opera "The Maiden Snang-sa" tells of the misfortunes of a peasant girl in Rgyal-rtse, based on a true incident well known to the people. The protagonists are ordinary men and women in real life, not the heroes and kings of historical legends or the goddesses and deities of mythological stories. The story of "Maiden Snang-sa" is as follows:

A beautiful, kind-hearted peasant girl named Snang-sa in Myang-stod (present-day Rgyal-rtse), in western Tibet, is spotted at a temple fair by Grags-chen-pa, a local lord. Through his power and position, he forces her to marry his son. Snang-sa's parents, intimidated by the local lord's authority, advise their daughter to submit to this. After her marriage she works hard all day long but is flogged and humiliated by the lord and his son. In consequence her ribs are broken and she dies of grief. After her death her soul comes back to the world and she becomes a nun. Later Grags-chen-pa and his son, educated by Buddhist teachings, are also converted to Buddhism.

With or without the religious element at the end, the story as a whole exposes the darkness of the feudal society and the brutal and despotic behavior of the local lord in a direct and effective way. Whenever it is performed, the actors and the audience merge into one and sobs are heard from many spectators.

The opera expresses deep sympathy for the laboring people, especially the toiling women. In portraying how maiden Snang-sa works, it says: "She gets up earlier than the cock at dawn, she goes to bed later than the old dog at night. She must roast highland barley, weave woolen fabric, work in the fields and be skilled at every job...." In a few lines, it brings out the rustic toil of a laboring woman. She is a gentle and industrious woman, but nevertheless she is doomed to a miserable destiny. The audience loves the opera, for they can readily identify themselves with Snang-sa. It is understandable that the lyrics of this opera reach all common people and they can sing them out of memory.

The opera "Don-yod and Don-grub" is also based on social customs. It focuses on a stepmother's mistreatment of the son of her husband's former wife, and love between two brothers. But later it was altered, shrouded in a religious mist, by the story of the previous incarnation of two Buddhist teachers. Hence, it lost its original luster.

The assimilation of stories of Buddhist scriptures into opera was somewhat related to its ties with the art of ballad singing. Among the Tibetans were ballad singers called Bla-ma-ma-ni, who specialized in telling stories from Buddhist scriptures. Their verses gradually developed from narration by a single performer to that of several actors singing their own parts, supplemented by another explaining the plot. Thus, Tibetan opera contains some pieces drawn from Buddhist sutras. The best-known of these is "Dri-med-kun-ldan." This piece describes how the prince sacrificed his own life so as to give alms to others and finally attained Buddhahood. The story is virtually the same as "The Crown Prince's Sudana Sutra in the Sayings of Buddha" in "Mahàvaipulya Sutra Tripitakas." This type of opera provides a valuable resource for studying the historical development of the dramatic tradition.

Tibetan opera uses simple, popular language, richly tinged with the witty diction and concise style of Tibetan literary language. Its use of metaphor is also characteristic of Tibetan literature. It is hoped that modern Tibetan opera will continue these traditions.

PRINCESS WENCHENG

Based on a folk legend, this drama is still popular in Tibet. A written record of it has been found in the literature of the 14th century. For example, "A Clear Mirror of the Pedigree of Tibetan Kings" by the Tibetan scholar Bsodnares Rgyalmtshan tells this story in great detail.

The plot is similar. This book was published in 1388. Another book, "A History of the Tibetan Kings and Ministers," published in 1643, also has this story, which is nearer to the current Tibetan drama.

Besides, the whole story of Princess Wencheng was portrayed in paintings with narrative sequence in Potala Palace murals handed down from the fifth generation of the Dalai Lama.

There are statues of Princess Wencheng in the Potala Palace and Dazhao Monastery in Tibet.

Many, many years ago, Btsan-po Srongb-tsan Sgam-po was born in Tibet. He grew up to become a prince of great talent and clever strategy. At the age of 16, he himself began to administer the land of Tibet.

The prince had a minister named Mgar Stongb-tsan Yul-srung, who was well-known as an able man among the Tibetan people.

One day Mgar said to Prince Srongb-tsan Sgam-po, "Emperor Tang Taizong has a princess who is endowed with the sixty-four abilities

17

and virtues* of an ideal woman. She is very beautiful, good and virtuous. She would be the best match for Your Majesty. We should send an envoy with presents to the emperor to propose marriage."

The prince was very glad. He appointed Minister Mgar special envoy for the purpose and ordered him to make preparations for the journey.

Mgar busied himself preparing presents, personnel, baggage, horses and camels. When everything was ready, he went and reported to the prince. The prince was pleased. He gave Mgar seven gold coins and said, "Present these gold coins to the emperor when you have an audience with him."

Then he took out an ancient suit of armor inlaid with agate, pearls, turquoises, as wells as red, blue, white, yellow and purple enamels. He said, "This precious armor will serve as a betrothal present."

The prince gave the minister three sealed envelopes, saying, "When you arrive at the Tang court, the emperor may question you closely. If you meet with difficulties, you could give him the envelopes in order, and what is written inside will help you answer all questions. Don't worry. You must be very careful during the journey and urge on your horses. When you come to steep mountains and turbulent rivers, you should silently pray to the Goddess of Mercy for her protection. Then misfortune will turn into blessing and you'll come safely out of danger."

On the eighth day of the fourth moon that year, which was an auspicious date, Mgar said goodbye to the Tibetan prince, to the other ministers and his family members and relatives and set out for

---

* The sixty-four abilities for the Tibetan ethnic group include appearance, useful arts, language and other virtues.

Chang'an, capital of the Tang Dynasty. He led a retinue of more than 100 people riding horses and camels and carrying all kinds of presents. They climbed mountains and forded rivers, overcoming countless difficulties and hardships. At last they arrived in the capital of the Tang Dynasty.

The procession entered Chang'an through the West Gate. It was a prosperous city with a population of hundreds of thousands. It took one day and one night to walk around the city wall. There were four majestic towers on top of the four gates on the north, south, east and west, spectacular buildings with carved beams and painted rafters. The buildings and street scenes evoked much admiration from Mgar and his men.

Meanwhile, envoys from other nations had also come to Chang'an to plead the cases of their princes or kings for the princess of the Tang emperor. The courting mission sent by the King of Buddhist India stayed in the eastern part of the city. The envoy of the prince of the military state of Gesar stayed in the southern part of the capital. The mission from the king of the wealthy state of Persia resided in the western part, while the envoy of the prince of the strong state of Tartar boarded in the northern part of the city. The Tibetan envoy stayed at a place between the northern and eastern parts. All the envoys tried to win an early audience with the emperor and to present him with strange and rich gifts.

The Tang emperor granted audience to the envoys one after another. The Tibetan envoy, however, was cold-shouldered with the reply: "Please wait a few days." One morning seven days later, clever Mgar saw the emperor come out of the palace riding in a carriage. He walked up to the emperor and presented him with the seven gold coins. He explained how the Tibetan prince admired the emperor's dignity and asked for the hand of the princess. Then he handed the armor to the emperor saying, "This is a unique armor. Whenever pestilence hits persons or livestock, Your Majesty could put it on and ride around the city, and the pestilence would immediately disappear. If any disasters of locusts, floods, hailstorms or drought take place, Your Majesty could put it on and ride around the fields, and the disasters would be held off. In case foreign invasion and war breaks out, Your Majesty could wear the armor and become invincible and all-conquering. This is a rare treasure, a state heirloom of Tibet. Prince Srongb-tsan Sgam-po has ordered me to present it to Your Majesty as a betrothal present, asking for the hand of the good and virtuous Princess of Wencheng."

Listening to the Tibetan envoy, the emperor disagreed with Mgar at heart, and his ministers around him thought the Tibetan prince had overstepped the ritual and was rash and ignorant. Giving a scornful laugh, the emperor said, "Since I succeeded to the throne of my late father, I've not done anything wrong or immoral. Your Tibetan prince is no match for me in both state power and territory. I don't expect he would venture to make such a request. You've come a long way and endured many hardships. I'm not going to blame you. Go back to Tibet promptly and ask Prince Srongb-tsan Sgam-po whether he can adopt the Ten Good Acts[*] as his administrative policies. If he can, I'll betroth the princess to him."

Hearing what the emperor said, Mgar replied, "To ask the prince a question, we have to go thousands of miles back to Tibet. It would waste time and delay a vital matter. It's fortunate, however, that our prince has prepared an answer to your question. It's in this envelope.

---

* The Ten Good Acts are the opposite of the Ten Evils.

Please open and read it." Then he handed the first envelope to the emperor.

The emperor opened the envelope. Inside was a message written in the Han language in letters of gold powder. The message read: "As people think the Tang emperor is an able statesman while the Tibetan prince is unable to rule by law, Your Majesty says if the Tibetan prince can adopt the Ten Good Acts as administrative policies, you would marry the princess to him. Very well. In my five thousand shapes, I'm carrying out the Ten Good Acts in a single day as my administrative policy. Please keep your word."

When he read the message, the emperor was surprised. Nevertheless, he pretended to be calm and leisurely. He said, "Ah! Your prince talks big. Good! Now you go quickly back to Tibet and ask Prince Srongb-tsan Sgam-po whether he can build halls of Buddhas in Tibet? If he can, I'll promise him the princess. If he can't, don't expect her to go to Tibet."

"Just for one question we would have to cover the long distance between here and Tibet," Mgar said. "When will we take the princess to Tibet? It's fortunate that our prince has already prepared an answer to your second question," and he handed the second envelope to the emperor.

The emperor opened the envelope. There was another message written in fine Han language. It read: "The Tang Dynasty has many skillful craftsmen, and the Buddhist doctrine is flourishing there. Halls of Buddhas are built everywhere. Therefore, Your Majesty says, 'If you can build halls of Buddhas, I'll promise you the princess.' Very good. I'm now ordering my five thousand shapes to build one hundred and eight great halls of Buddhas, each with its entrance facing the Tang court. Please don't break your promise."

The emperor was astonished. Pretending to be calm, he said, "Your prince is a braggart. Very well. Now go back immediately and ask Prince Srongb-tsan Sgam-po whether there are plenty of goods in Tibet for the five senses to enjoy. If there are, he can take the princess' hand. If there is none, how can I let him have the princess?"

"It's unnecessary for us to cover thousands of miles to and fro to find an answer to Your Majesty's question," Mgar said. "The answer is already here." He gave the third envelope to the emperor.

The emperor opened the third envelope and read the message. It read: "People always say the Tang Dynasty is rich and prosperous while Tibet is poor and destitute. Therefore, Your Majesty says if Tibet has plenty of property for the five senses to enjoy, you would promise me the princess. Very well. I'm ordering my five thousand shapes to prepare gold, silver, silks, clothing, food grain, ornaments and other things. All these shall be exquisitely made as if by God. Meanwhile, we'll open a gate in each of the four directions so that the wealth of other parts of the world can flow into our state. In a short time, we will become a rich, powerful and invincible nation. Is this a surprise to Your Majesty?"

After reading the message, the emperor felt puzzled and depressed. He returned to his palace.

The emperor gathered the queen, prince and princess to discuss what should they do, which state the princess should be married to.

The emperor said, "Some ministers say Buddhism came from India, and Buddha shows kindness to all our people. Therefore, we should marry our princess to India. I think they are well founded."

The queen was a stingy and avaricious person. She said, "Persia is a powerful and wealthy state where the ground is covered by gold and silver and the cities are full of pearls and treasures. Our princess will enjoy all her life if she is married there."

The prince was a brave man who loved the martial arts. He said, "The Tartars are a powerful nation. If we are linked with them by marriage, it will greatly increase the power of our state."

The princess herself, however, wanted to choose a handsome and strong man to be her lifelong companion. She preferred Prince Gesar.

Not one of them said a word about the Tibetan prince.

The emperor could not come to a conclusion. So he summoned all envoys of the courting states and said: "You envoys have made a long, tiring journey to Chang'an. Now, I can't decide which state I should marry my princess to. The only way to reach a decision is to test your wisdom. Please be attentive."

The Tang emperor took out a crystal-clear and sparkling jade pearl and a red silk thread. He said, "There is a tiny passage with nine bends going through this pearl. Whoever threads the pearl with the red silk will win the princess for his prince."

All the envoys tried hard to put the red silk thread through the pearl. Half a day passed by, but none succeeded. At last they passed the pearl to Mgar. As the wise Tibetan envoy surveyed the pearl carefully, he saw a little ant crawling on the ground. He picked up the ant, tied the red silk around its waist, then put it into the hole of the pearl. He blew softly at the ant while placing a little honey at the other end of the hole. Lured by the flavor of the honey and forced by his breath, the ant crawled ahead through the tunnel to the other end, carrying the red silk thread with it.

The Tibetan envoy brought the threaded pearl to the emperor and asked him to marry the princess to the Tibetan prince.

The emperor muttered to himself, unable to make up his mind. Then he said, "Although you won the competition this time, I can't make a careless decision. You have to compete a second time."

The next day the emperor ordered his men to bring 500 goats to the meeting place. He said to the five envoys, "Now each of you take a hundred goats. In a single day tomorrow, your mission is to butcher all one hundred goats, eat all the meat and turn all the goatskins into leather. Whoever succeeds will have the princess."

Bringing back his 100 goats, Mgar told each of his 100-member entourage to slaughter a goat and skin it. Then they put the skins in one pile and the mutton in another pile. Mgar ordered his 100 men to sit in a circle. One man was to cut the mutton into pieces as big as a walnut, which were cooked and passed around. In turn each man put a little salt on a piece of mutton and ate it. As the mutton pieces were passed around the circle, the men ate them little by little and finished all the mutton in the afternoon. Then the 100 goatskins were passed around one by one. Each man took turns rubbing each goatskin three times. When a goatskin came to the end of the line, it had been rubbed into leather. In this way the hundred goatskins were quickly turned into leather.

When Mgar brought the leather before the emperor, the other envoys were still busy eating mutton or rubbing goatskins. Some had not even butchered their last goat.

Mgar said to the emperor, "We've slaughtered our hundred goats, eaten all mutton and turned all goatskins into leather according to Your Majesty's order. Please marry the princess to our prince."

The emperor wondered in his heart. But he said, "No. I mustn't carelessly marry the princess to your prince. I'll hold another contest tomorrow."

The next day the emperor ordered 100 mares and 100 foals to be brought. He said to all the envoys, "Whoever matches up each mare with her foal can have the princess."

The envoys stared at each other, not knowing what to do. Only Mgar stepped forward and said, "I can do it."

He tethered the 100 foals in stables so that they could not see the mares. He gave the foals neither fodder nor water throughout the night. The next morning he brought them before the mares. Hungry and thirsty, each foal eagerly looked for its mother to suck her milk. Each pair was clearly matched this way.

Mgar reported to the emperor. Nevertheless, the emperor said, "I must be very careful. Please come to another competition tomorrow."

Next morning, the emperor ordered men to bring 100 logs, each having the same diameter at both ends. He said to the envoys, "Each of these 100 logs was sawn off so that both ends have the same diameter. Whoever can tell which end is nearer to the roots of the tree will have the princess."

The envoys looked at the logs, turned them this way and that, stroked them, and weighed them in their hands. No one could tell which end of any log was nearer to the roots. Mgar thought for a while, then told his men to take the 100 logs to the riverbank. They threw the logs into the river. Floating on water, the end nearer the roots dipped lower than the other end because it was slightly heavier. Thus, Mgar could tell which end of a log was nearer to the roots.

Reporting to the emperor, Mgar said, "I've distinguished each end of every one of the logs. Please don't go back on your word again— marry the princess to our prince."

Nevertheless, the emperor said, "I've made a final decision. Three days from now I'll gather three hundred beauties at the East Drill Ground. They shall put on the same dresses and ornaments. Among them will be my princess. Whoever succeeds in singling her out will have her to marry to his prince. This is the last contest. I'll not break my word."

Hearing this, Mgar was sad. He returned to his lodgings, feeling gloomy. He thought aloud, "We came a long way from Lhasa to Chang'an, enduring thousands of hardships. We met the Tang emperor and thought we could successfully take the princess back to Tibet. Nevertheless, we have met with many obstacles. Our Tibetan prince is a blessed man, and we have won the competition time and again. Now we will have the last contest at the East Drill Ground three days from now. If we fail to single out the princess, a proverb will come true which says, 'The crane is all white except a black spot on the tip of its tail.' We must bring all our energy and wisdom into play in the final competition."

As he was worrying, the old woman-servant of the inn came up and said, "Why does our honorable guest look so sad today?"

Mgar told her what was on his mind. "Alas, we've overcome untold hardships coming to Chang'an," he said. "We thought we could quickly escort Princess Wencheng to Tibet to marry our prince. The Tang emperor, however, has put one obstacle after another in our way. It's fortunate that we have won every competition so far. There's a saying: 'A word said is like a slashing sword, or flowing water, or a galloping horse.' One should not hold it back. But the emperor went back on his word and has asked us to pick out the princess from three hundred beauties, three days from now. We have only heard that the princess is beautiful and virtuous, charming and cultured. We've never met her. Now, the three hundred beauties are of the same stature and dressed the same way. How can we single out the princess? We will fail this time! You've worked hard serving us, but for nothing! How could it not worry me and make me sad?"

"No worry," the old woman-servant said. "I think His Majesty himself would not look down on you. It's his ministers who have no favorable impression of you. I could help you, but I'm afraid...."

Sensing something important in her words, Mgar coaxed her, saying, "We've been together for months. Don't you know us well? Why should you be afraid? Please help us!"

"I know very well you are honest and sincere men," she said. "It's the best thing for our princess to marry your prince. I've worked decades in the palace since childhood, serving many princesses and maids of honor. I have loved and respected Princess Wencheng best of all. I attended her for years, and I'll never forget her look and manners. It's easy for me to tell you her features. But there's an adviser in the imperial court who can tell fortunes. No secret can escape him. If one day he tells my fortune and finds out that I've leaked out the secret, It'll be hard for me to preserve my life."

"We're grateful to you for your kindness," Mgar said. "In any case you must help us this time. You'll get whatever reward you want. We've heard of that adviser. Nevertheless, you needn't be afraid. I've a way to make him fail to tell who informs us of the princess' characteristics."

"Honorable guest," the woman-servant said, "please listen attentively. The princess has cheeks glowing with health, superbly blending white and pink. Her body emits a faint fragrance. There's always a bee flying about her face, which looks like a lotus flower in full bloom. A red mole dots the spot between her eyebrows. According to the custom of the palace, the princess will stand neither at the head of the line nor at its end. She always counts sixth from bottom up on the left row. Her dress is made of lustrous and slippery fabric, which is hard to catch hold of. You'd better bend an arrow into a hook and tie it with a silk thread. When you're certain it's the princess, just put the hook on her silk coat and you're sure of success."

Mgar was overjoyed. He promptly assembled his entourage and said, "Brothers, we've come to Chang'an neither to do business for profit nor to preach Buddhism. We come especially for Princess Wencheng. We've won the previous competitions, thanks to your concerted efforts. Once again I have to rely on you for final victory in the last contest. We must bear in mind the special features of the princess and single her out three days from now. We have to succeed in this important matter!"

Three days passed. On the appointed day the whole city turned out to watch the bustling scene. Three hundred beauties, gorgeously dressed, stood in line on the East Drill Ground, dazzling and fascinating all the spectators.

The emperor gave the order: "Let all the envoys come up in order to pick out the princess!"

The envoy from India was the first to try. He carefully looked at each beauty from the head of the line until he came to the middle of the line. He picked out two girls and insisted that one of them must be the princess. Happily, he led the two beauties away.

Then came the envoys from Persia, Gesar and Tartar, one after the other. Each of them also picked out two beauties and led them away. All the time Mgar, the Tibetan envoy, was nervously watching them picking out beauties. When he saw that all other envoys failed to recognize the princess, he heaved a sigh of relief and could not help laughing. He hurried onto the drill ground with his men and surveyed each beauty carefully from the top to the bottom of the line. Then he counted the girls from the lowest line up to number six. Looking at the beauty before him for a while, he said: "Are you not Princess

Wencheng who is the incarnation of the Goddess? Your face is glowing with health. Your skin is tinged with a superb blend of pink and white and is smooth as ivory. Your body emits a strange fragrance. Your cheeks are like a blooming lotus flower, and a bee is always humming near you. This is no other person than Princess Wencheng herself!"

Mgar threw out his hook, which caught hold of the collar of the princess' coat. Seeing that her identity had been revealed, the princess began to cry.

The Tibetan envoy had achieved his aim. The worry he had suffered many days turned into happiness. Leading the princess along, he began to sing. Two of his men blew flutes in accompaniment. Mgar sang:

Our honorable princess,
Beautiful fairy maiden;
Please listen to my message,
Do not worry and sadden.
Tibet is a vast area,
Where the five treasures are found.
The Tibetan prince is wise,
And he is kind at heart.
Everyone admires him.
The whole nation sings of peace.
There are ten thousand kinds of trees in the mountains;
There are vast grasslands and beautiful plains.
All five kinds of grains and six kinds of beans thrive there.
Gold, silver, copper, iron and tin are found.
Cattle and sheep dot the hillsides;
Silks and satins fill storehouses.
Peace prevails in the good land;

People enjoy happiness.
Let the princess hear this message,
And think it over carefully.

Listening to Mgar's song, the princess thought: "His words show that there is not much difference between Tibet and our Tang kingdom." This somewhat relieved her fears. Wiping her tears away, she walked slowly following the Tibetan envoy.

Mgar said to the other envoys, "Now that we've won the princess, we're soon going back to Tibet. Please come and see us off!"

Mgar brought horses and urged the princess to ride. They rode through the main thoroughfares of the city to demonstrate the wisdom, ability and victory of the Tibetan people.

All the residents of Chang'an acknowledged that it was the greatest event ever in the city. Some sighed at the lot of the princess. Others praised her.

Seeing that the real princess had been picked out by the Tibetan envoy, Emperor Tang Taizong said to the other envoys, "The princess is going to marry the Tibetan prince. You can also take home the beauties you've chosen. We are related to them by marriage too."

It couldn't be helped. The envoys were content to take home the beauties they had picked.

Mgar asked the princess to return to the Tang palace to pack up her things for the journey.

Back in the palace, the emperor said to the princess, "My darling, you'll be married to the Tibetan prince as his queen. You must take good care of yourself."

"Tibet is very, very far away," the princess replied. "It's hard not to see Father and Mother again! I don't want to go."

"Don't talk nonsense," the emperor said. "You know the Tibetan prince is a man of remarkable ability who has mastered magical power. When I questioned his envoy, the prince had already prepared the answers. Without the trouble of taking a step, his envoy answered all my questions one after the other. I think all the Tibetans are very clever and smart. It's good for you to marry the prince there."

Kneeling before the emperor, the princess said, "I understand Father's order, Mother's persuasion and Brother's guidance. Nevertheless, it's said that Tibet is covered with snow and is ice-bound all the year round. The snow mountains there look like the fangs of beasts of prey. Rocks loom like the horns of wild bulls. No grain can grow there, and the people are starving. The Tibetans do not believe in Buddha, and there is not a single temple in the state. There's no place to cultivate goodness and benefit people. What should I place my hope on when I go there? If you want me to marry the Tibetan prince, please give me the statue of Buddha Sakyamuni you are worshipping, so that I can pray to Buddha in the morning and evening. Besides, please grant me seeds of food grain, fabrics for clothing, as well as maids and servants, so that I can turn a poor and desolate territory into fertile and wealthy land."

As she said this, tears streamed down the princess' cheeks and she sobbed.

The emperor was sad too. He comforted her saying, "Although snow often falls in Tibet, the snow mountains are like natural pagodas storing treasures. Tibet is surrounded by seas and when the strange golden flowers bloom, you'll enjoy a magnificent scene. There are four major rivers irrigating the territory, with dense and luxuriant forests. Like white clouds, sheep and cattle cover the plains and mountain slopes. The Tibetan prince is characterized by his benevolence. He bans the Ten Evils* and cultivates the Ten Good Acts. All the citizens are wise, and the ministers are able and virtuous persons.

"I'll let you keep Buddha's statue, which was made of ten kinds of precious material by Visvakarma, the founder of all arts, according to a painting by Brgyabyin, the Buddhist Creator. I've cherished it as my greatest treasure. Now you have it. In our treasure house there is something I like best, a bookcase inlaid with gold and jades. Take it as your dowry. In addition, take to Tibet three hundred and sixty kinds of artifacts, including gold and jade utensils, as well as food, beverages, silks, satins and patterns for making various wonderful things. They are my gifts. Then take with you three hundred copies of Han poems, sixty copies of warning mottos, two hundred and forty prescriptions for curing diseases, twenty thousand bolts of silk and satin, and twenty-five maids.

"My darling, I want you ever to bear in mind these words of mine: 'Handle matters fairly, speak peacefully, treat all persons alike, love your subjects, respect the Tibetan prince, and never overstep rules and regulations in your actions.'"

The princess tightly held the emperor's hands in hers. They were reluctant to part from each other. At this juncture, Mgar came and urged the princess to set out for Tibet. The magnitude of the trousseau of the princess was beyond Mgar's expectations. His mission took a long time loading her treasures, clothing, ornaments, food and seed grain on camels and horses. They put the statue of Buddha in a flower-decked carriage driven by two men of unusual strength.

The emperor invited the Tibetan mission to a farewell party,

---

* The Ten Evils are murder, stealing, lewdness, recklessness, fine phrases, foul-mouthed language, double-tongued behavior, anger, avarice and wicked ideas.

with theatrical performances. After wine was passed around a few times, Princess Wencheng, charmingly dressed in silk robes and jade ornaments, arrived and kowtowed to the emperor and queen, bidding farewell to them.

The emperor said, "If my darling praises and spreads Buddhism in Tibet, you'll perform boundless beneficence. This will be your religious merit."

The emperor, queen, prince and all the high officials and generals of the imperial court, as well as countless citizens, saw the princess off outside the gate of the capital. Saying goodbye to all, the princess and her maids and servants rode on horses with the Tibetan envoy and went west, leading a mighty convoy.

PRINCE NOR-BZANG

This opera has been adapted from a folk myth. Under the title "Nor-bzang's Romance," the story was first recorded in the book "Fabulous Tree Capable of Responding to Every Wish." It had virtually the same episodes.

Later, Tshe-ring-dbang-rgyal thought that "Nor-bzang's Romance," restricted by archaic expressions and rhyme, was not adaptable for acting and singing. He began the adaptation into the opera "Prince Nor-bzang" in its present form. But, judging by the data recorded in "History of Ministers in Tibet," the adaptation and performance must have been completed at the latest at the time of Ngag-dbang-blo-bzang-rgya-mtsbo (1617-1682), who was author of the above-mentioned book. The story of this opera has also been quoted in the love songs written by Tshangs-dbyangs-rgya-mtsbo (1683-1705).

Long, long ago, there were two countries. The southern country was named Rig-dan-pa, and the northern country was Sngags-ldan-pa. At first, the two countries had about the same amount of land, people and natural resources, and all led a happy and comfortable life.

But a new king named Zhag-pa-gzhon-nu began to rule the southern country. He was an ambitious tyrant: greedy, despotic and cruel. He made the country fall into disintegration. Crop failures occurred and many people fled elsewhere. Things went from bad to worse. Even the king felt something was wrong, and worried much about it.

One day, the king assembled his ministers to study the reason for the decline of the country. Some ministers spoke of the benevolence of King Nor-chen and Prince Nor-bzang in Sngags-ldan-pa, the northern country, and how they enjoyed great popularity among their people. Some ministers pointed out King Zhag-pa-gzhon-nu's many defects in the past and how this made him lose popularity among his people and brought about the wrath of heaven and the resentment of men. Some other ministers advised the king to carry out more benevolent policies. But instead of heeding their opinions, the king was offended.

At that time, a particularly vicious minister said: "The cause of the decline of our country is that our magic dragons moved to the Pad-ma-bla-mtsbo Lake, in the northern country. Since big dragon, small dragon and their dragon sons and grandsons moved there, with each passing day we have become more unlucky. Now, the only thing to do is to invite several sorcerers with great supernatural powers to use their art to bring the magic dragons back to our country and let them live in Bla-mbho Lake, as before. Then our country will surely turn from weakness to strength, and from decline to prosperity."

After hearing these words, the king was much encouraged and nodded his approval. That very night, he sent emissaries deep into the hills to invite a sorcerer to capture the dragons. The sorcerer who accepted the invitation was Gru-na-kha-vdzin, the country's foremost master of magic arts. He was skilled at swallowing knives, spitting fire, and rising into the clouds and mist. Gathering his disciples and the paraphernalia of his black arts, the sorcerer went stealthily to the bank of the Pad-ma-bla-mtsbo Lake in the northern country of Sngags-ldan-pa to capture the dragons.

At this moment, the dragon god, knowing that a disaster was about to befall him, transformed himself into a child and emerged from the surface of the lake. He asked Spang-legs-byin-pa, a hunter who lived beside the lake, to help him, saying, "Tomorrow, in the evening of the fifteenth day of the fourth month, a sorcerer from the southern country of Rig-ldan-pa will come here to capture the dragon god. Pray help us to defeat him."

The hunter said, "I'll surely come to help the dragon god. Hunting and fishing are the professions handed down from our forefathers. All our family's livelihood depends on the protection of the dragon god." He sharpened his knife at home, in preparation for battle.

The next evening when the moon was rising, the sorcerer from the southern country arrived at the lake. First, he embedded eight iron pillars around the four sides of the lake, and placed a silk canopy over the pillars. Then he scattered filthy blood and water and other poisons into the lake, while murmuring incantations. Soon the lake water was seething like a boiling pot and an offensive smell rose up to the sky.

The dragon gods could no longer stay in the lake. They came out of its surface one by one and fought desperately with the sorcerer. But they could not hold out against him. Just then, the hunter came to the edge of the lake and, seizing the sorcerer by the collarbone so that he could not move, ordered him to withdraw his magic and let the dragon gods return to the lake. In the end, he killed the sorcerer with his knife and chased away the disciples. Only then did the lake become calm again.

To show their gratitude, the dragon gods presented the hunter with an object of treasure, called Bsamvphel, a symbol of good luck. The hunter took it home and asked his neighbors, an old couple, about the use of this object. They did not know how to use it either, and advised him to go to Ga-vu-ri-khrod Mountain cave to inquire about it from a hermit who was undergoing Buddhist discipline there. The hermit, Blo-gros-rig-gsal, was an old man of profound attainment. He had been an ascetic Buddhist for many years in the cave, and had no thought for worldly affairs.

When the hunter came into his presence and showed him the treasure, the hermit was greatly astonished and asked, "Where did the treasure come from?" The hunter recounted how he had helped the dragon gods defeat the enemy sorcerer and how they had rewarded him with the treasure.

The hermit told the hunter that the treasure was called Bsam-vphel, and that it was a symbol of good luck. Whoever possessed it would immediately become the wealthiest man in the land and his family would never have to worry about food or clothing. The hunter was very happy. Later, he asked the hermit how he had lived to such an advanced age. The hermit said, "I have lived so long because I often bathe in a fairy lake."

The lake was behind the hill where the hermit lived. This fairy lake was pure, shining as a mirror, and reflected all the three thousand boundless universes at its bottom. Beside the lake were flowers that never faded through all the seasons and grasses that were always green. A hundred birds sang in sweet, melodious tones and the David's deer roamed along the banks. The hunter accompanied the hermit through the woods beside the lake.

In the deep, quiet evening in this mountain valley, seven moons appeared. Suddenly, seven beautiful fairy maidens were bathing merrily in the lake, their frolicking spraying lake water in all directions. Their pure, fair skin sparkled in the droplets of water. As he watched this enchanting scene, the hunter asked the hermit where the maidens came from.

"These maidens live in the heavens," said the hermit. "They are the daughters of a celestial musician and fly to this world only to bathe in the fairy lake. Their leader is Yid-vphrog-lha-mo. She is queen of these maidens."

The hunter gazed at the lake infatuated, and did not want to leave. He stayed until dawn, when the seven fairy maidens finished bathing and put on thin silk gauze and, like seven white cranes, flew back to the celestial musician's heavenly palace. (This musician, their father, was a being somewhat between a god and a human, called "the one who seeks fragrance.")

Only when the maidens had gone did the hunter feel he had regained consciousness, and returned with the hermit to the mountain cave. On the way, he begged the hermit: "Great lama with profound attainment and infinite power, pray find a way that I can marry the fairy maiden Yid-vphrog-lha-mo! She is so beautiful, so sweet, so gentle and so quiet!"

The hermit laughed and said, "It's not easy! She is a fairy maiden and can fly up to the heavens in the daytime. How could you prevent her from leaving you?"

The hunter said, "Don't I have the treasure Bsam-vphel? With its power, can't I stop her and keep her as my life partner?"

The hermit shook his head. "No, that won't work. Bsam-vphel is indeed a treasure of good luck, but it only provides wealth and plenty of food and clothing. How can it prevent the fairy maiden from going away?" But the hunter kept entreating, and finally the hermit said, "As far as I know, the dragon king in the Pad-ma-bla-mtsho Lake has a treasure called 'fairy-tying rope.' If you obtain it, you can prevent the fairy maiden from going away."

"The Pad-ma-bla-mtsho Lake is in my native land, and the dragon

38

king is the one whose life I saved just a few days ago. Let me go and consult with him," said the hunter, and ran off towards the Pad-ma-bla-mtsbo Lake without looking back.

When he came to the lake, the hunter, with the Bsam-vphel treasure in his hand, called to the dragon king and asked him to come out. The dragon king emerged and saw it was the hunter who had saved his life. "Heroic warrior, what instructions do you have?" the dragon asked the hunter.

"The treasure Bsam-vphel that you gave me is of no use to me, a hunter. Let me return it to you." The dragon king was astonished. "The Bsam-vphel is a precious object in the dragon palace," he said. "It can turn you into a man of great wealth at once. Why don't you want it anymore?"

The hunter said, "I do not want wealth. If you still remember my kindness, pray lend me the fairy-tying rope. I will always be grateful to you."

But because the rope was a treasure that guarded the lakes and kept them secure, he could not lend it to others. The dragon king was in a dilemma because the hunter had saved his life and was his benefactor, and he did not want to refuse. So he said, "I can lend you the fairy-tying rope, but you must make a solemn pledge not to tie the children and grandchildren of the dragons, not to tie the deities and Buddhas, and not to tie the celestial musicians."

The hunter listened and answered: "Words spoken are like arrows shot from the bow. Open-hearted men will not be underhanded. I promise not to tie the children and grandchildren of the dragons, and not to tie the deities and the Buddhas. But I cannot promise not to tie the celestial musicians. If it were not for the daughter of a celestial musician, why would I borrow this fairy-tying rope? Lend it to me if

39

you are willing; let it be if you are unwilling."

Seeing that the hunter had grown angry, the dragon king made haste to say, "Well, I will lend it to you." He went back at once to the dragon palace, took out a small rope emitting five-colored rays, and gave it to the hunter.

The hunter, having obtained the fairy-tying rope, hurried back to the Ga-vu-ri-khrod Mountain cave to get the hermit to think of a way for him to secure the maiden. The hermit, fearing the hunter would make trouble with the fairy-tying rope, would not allow him to return to the lake, but went alone. But the hunter stealthily followed and hid himself in the dense woods at the side of the lake. He waited until deep in the night when the moon shone brightly, the breeze was gentle, and all was quiet.

The seven fairy maidens came again to bathe in the lake. The hunter, barely breathing, took the fairy-tying rope in one hand, and waited until the moment when they put on their silk gauze and began to fly up to the heavens. Then he threw the rope towards the most beautiful of the maidens, Yid-vphrog-lha-mo. The others were enjoying themselves, never imagining that Yid-vphrog-lha-mo would be tightly tied by a rope that had flown over her. She was unable to move even a tiny bit, and fell straight down to the bank of the lake. The other six maidens were panic-stricken, not knowing what had happened, and flew to and fro and circled above her.

When the hunter saw that the rope really brought the fairy maiden down, he was overjoyed and rushed over to her. The hermit, standing at one side, also saw what had happened and hurried there at the same time. The hunter, pulling one end of the rope, drew the maiden slowly into his arms. She, unable to control her movements, bashfully came to his side. The hunter said joyfully: "Fairy maiden in heaven, beautiful fairy maiden, at last you have fallen down to this world. I have fulfilled my lifelong wish. Let us together thank the deities and the Buddhas for their protection."

But the fairy maiden entreated him: "Brave warrior, vigorous hunter, pray set me free. I can pay you as much money as you ask. I can give you any treasure you want. Pray set me free!"

The hunter raised his face and laughed. "I want neither money nor treasure. For your sake, fairy maiden, I have given up the treasure Bsam-vphel. This is an auspicious day. Let us thank heaven." With these words, he slowly drew the rope tightly about her. As they saw this, the six fairy maidens circling in the sky shouted, "Pitiful elder sister, flower in the hearts of Father and Mother! Why have you been so unlucky as to fall into a trap? How can we leave you alone?"

The fairy maiden Yid-vphrog-lha-mo raised her head and sobbed: "Younger sisters, the bad luck of this year and this month has brought me this disaster. Fly back quickly to our parents and beg them to send jewels for my ransom!"

To the fairy maidens in the sky, the hunter called: "Little maidens, go quickly to tell your parents that Yid-vphrog-lha-mo has been captured by me and no matter how many treasures you bring, you cannot ransom her. But if you wish to provide her dowry, I won't refuse the gift."

The six fairy maidens again circled the sky, then with a long whistling sound, flew straight to the celestial musician's house. The hunter drew the fairy-tying rope tighter and tighter, until the maiden found it hard to breathe. The hermit came forward to her aid, advising the hunter to loosen the rope. The hunter said, "It is quite difficult for me to secure the maiden. If I loosen the rope, she will fly into the heavens, and what will I do then? Can you take the responsibility of returning her to me?"

The hermit told the fairy maiden to take the pearl necklace from her neck and give it to the hunter, and said, "Now she has handed over to you the pearl necklace which gives her the strength to fly up to heaven. She can no longer fly away. You can unfasten the fairy-tying rope. Let us earnestly decide how to handle this matter; otherwise, her life is in danger!"

The hunter took the necklace and unfastened the fairy-tying rope. The poor thing had been tied so tightly that she looked like a sun-withered flower, and was very feeble and on the verge of death. The hunter again tried to compel her to agree to stay with him. Over and over, she asked the hermit for help. He pondered this for a long while, and then turned to speak to the hunter: "Brave hunter, stalwart warrior, pray listen to a few words from me. This fairy maiden, Yid-vphrog-lha-mo, is a descendant of a celestial musician and absolutely cannot marry a hunter. If she did so, it would bring about disaster and death, and this would be of no good to you, to her, or to anybody. Our Prince Nor-bzang is the reincarnation of a Buddha. He is benevolent and generous to people, industrious, and leads a thrifty and simple life. If you present the fairy maiden to him, it would bring the greatest happiness to our whole country."

The hunter, realizing that the fairy maiden would rather die than consent to marry him, was willing to obey the hermit's instructions. Therefore, he promised straightforwardly to present the fairy maiden to Prince Nor-bzang.

When the fairy maiden Yid-vphrog-lha-mo and the hunter left to go to the palace, the hermit escorted them for a while, and then said, "Go straight to Prince Nor-bzang's palace, Dgav-bavi-bsam-gling, both of you! You must keep your vow and present the fairy maiden and her necklace to the prince. From my oracle I have divined that they two were predestined for marriage, from a previous incarnation."

At the entrance to the palace stood rows of impressive warriors. The hunter stepped forward and asked for an audience with the prince. The warriors reported to a palace courtier, who at once told Prince Nor-bzang, "Outside is a hunter leading a beautiful maiden. He requests an audience with you." The prince said, "Ah ha. They've come indeed. Last night I had a dream in which I had a bouquet of flowers in my hand. Surely this coincides with their arrival. Hasten to call them in."

The hunter led the fairy maiden into the courtyard and was received by Prince Nord-bzang in an exquisite palace. The hunter explained what he knew about the fairy maiden, and about his own situation. He also told the prince he was presenting the fairy maiden to him in accordance with the hermit's instructions. The prince rejoiced in the loyalty of the hunter, who had undergone such hardship to obtain the fairy maiden and present her to him,* and he was struck by the beauty of the maiden.

The prince himself sat on a block of gold, the fairy maiden on a block of silver, and the hunter on a damask block covered with tiger skin. He ordered lavish banquets to celebrate the occasion with his ministers and the people.

At this time, auspicious clouds of five colors appeared in the sky and wonderful music was heard in the air. Flowers as lovely as rosy clouds were raining down. The prince was extraordinarily pleased. He conferred the title of princess on Yid-vphrog-lha-mo and gave great

---

* However, a Tibetan folk ballad presents a different story, which says: "Beloved Yid-vphrog-lha-mo was captured by me, the hunter, but was taken away by force by Prince Nor-bzang, a powerful tyrant."

rewards to the hunter and bade him return to his home.

On the twentieth day of the eighth month, in the year of the local dragon, great banners were hung and conches were blown. The prince assembled officials and people from all over the country for a grand wedding celebration. There were horse racing, archery contests, waving flags and beating drums. All the people rejoiced that the fairy maiden had come to the palace.

After Prince Nor-bzang married the fairy maiden Yid-vphrog-lha-mo, he forgot all about the 500 imperial concubines. He was in her company all day long and they were as inseparable as body and soul. He said, "At the sight of Yid-vphrog-lha-mo, all the sorrow and melancholy of three incarnations are immediately driven away." Yid-vphrog-lha-mo loved the prince just as deeply, and led the happiest life in this world.

All was well until their deep love aroused the jealousy of the 500 imperial concubines. At first, they talked of Yid-vphrog-lha-mo's dubious background in the prince's presence, but he did not pay any attention. Then they spread rumors in and outside the palace about how ugly and cruel Yid-vphrog-lha-mo was. But people had seen the fairy maiden and they had received her alms.

Finally, the concubines held a meeting, and one of them, Don-grub-pad-ma, offered a scheme: to ask the old king's sorcerer, He-ra, a crafty, vicious fellow, to use magic art to suppress the fairy maiden. In ordinary times, He-ra made trouble out of nothing, always afraid that the country would lack chaos. When the imperial concubines brought treasure and money and asked for help, he was overjoyed. He readily agreed to their request and promised to find a way to kill Yid-vphrog-lha-mo, so that they would regain the prince's favor. The concubines said if he succeeded, they would give him the same amount as that bestowed on the hunter when he presented Yid-vphrog-lha-mo to the prince.

From then on, the old king was awakened by nightmares several nights in a row. One night in particular, he dreamed that many vicious wolves suddenly came into the midst of a flock of sheep and bit them to death one by one, and seized several of the sheep's heads in their mouths. The old king was so shocked that he was in a cold sweat. When he awoke, he quickly assembled his ministers to have the dream explained. They all said it was an evil omen but that they could not tell what it really meant. Then He-ra came forward, saying: "Your Majesty, this is an evil omen, and an unusual one. Let me consult my oracle to see what the deities' instructions are."

He-ra put up a white wool blanket and sprayed white powder, wine and water all over it. Then he took a bronze bell in his right hand and a small drum of human bones in his left hand and murmured these words while striking the bell and beating the drum: "Powerful savages live in the northern wilderness. Now they are bringing their troops to stage a rebellion. If we don't send our finest troops to launch an offensive, our country will fall into ruin and people will die next year."

Hearing these words, old King Nor-chen believed in them, and became panic-stricken and pale. Quickly he asked the ministers: "Who can lead our best troops to fight in the distant northern wilderness, defeat the enemy and defend our country?" He asked this three times in a row, but the ministers looked at each other in dismay, and none of them uttered a word. The old king gave a long sigh and tears streamed down his face.

At this time, the sorcerer He-ra offered a scheme: "Your Majesty, pray don't worry. Why don't you send Prince Nor-bzang there? I imagine the northern troops are only silly buffoons and will be easily

45

vanquished by our heavenly troops. Besides, the prince is famous for his military exploits far and near. Surely he will win an immediate victory." So the old king ordered Prince Nor-bzang to lead special troops to fight against the distant northern country. Prince Nor-bzang vowed: "For the sake of defending our country; for the order of my father, the king; and for the heroic task, I will surely lead the troops against the distant northern country!'

"But," he added, "my father, pray allow me to take Yid-vphrog-lha-mo along. She can advise me in military affairs and share my worries and strenuous work. This will be beneficial to both of us."

The sorcerer He-ra said, "Your Majesty, you must never allow the prince to take a woman along. It would be a great disadvantage to both the country and the prince. It would also endanger her life." Believing in the sorcerer's words, the king did not allow the prince to take Yid-vphrog-lha-mo along.

The news of the prince's going to fight against the distant northern country spread through the palace. The prince's mother and the fairy maiden Yid-vphrog-lha-mo were very distressed. Holding their heads in their hands, the two women sobbed unceasingly and were in deep sorrow. Prince Nor-bzang went to his mother and entreated her: "To defend our country and obey my father, the king, I will go to the far northern wilderness. But I am worried about Yid-vphrog-lha-mo. She is the target of the jealousy of the imperial concubines and is in a very difficult situation. Mother, pray give her special protection." With these words, he took out the necklace the hunter had given him, and gave it to his mother. He said, "This necklace represents her wings, with it she can fly up into the heavens. You must never let her return to her heavenly palace unless her life is in danger. Otherwise, when I return, I will expect you to give her back to me."

At this time, the fairy maiden Yid-vphrog-lha-mo at their side was weeping so bitterly that she was wet with tears. The mother advised her son to set his heart at ease and her daughter-in-law not to worry. She herself tried to keep her spirits high and get wine and food ready to send off the prince and the troops.

To the prince and Yid-vphrog-lha-mo, it seemed as though this one miserable day lasted longer than a year and their one happy year had been shorter than a day. They were deeply distressed and found it difficult to part from each other. But the king's order was like a stone rolled down from a high mountain, which could never roll up again. It was like a stream flowing down from a river, that could never flow up again.

Finally, the day arrived for marching off to battle. The ministers and the commoners toasted the prince with the first glass of wine, wishing him early victory and a safe return. The 500 imperial concubines made the second toast, wishing him victory and success. Yid-vphrog-lha-mo made the third toast, conveying thousands of words and tender feelings with her tears. Then, leading his solemn, impressive troops to brave a world of ice and snow, the heroic Prince Nor-bzang marched off to the northern wilderness.

Prince Nor-bzang was gone and the first step of the sorcerer's intrigue was carried out. It was time for the second step in He-ra's nefarious activities.

Old King Nor-chen had nightmares several nights in succession. He dreamed that Prince Nor-bzang had ridden off on horseback to the northern wilderness. Suddenly, many soldiers came to the palace and encircled it, ring upon ring, tied up Nor-chen and carried him off, and he met a very horrible end. When he awakened he was in a cold sweat and his heart was pounding. The sorcerer He-ra was called in to consult his oracle and predict whether the dream was good luck or a bad omen. The sorcerer, as before, went through an elaborate ritual, placed offerings and kowtowed, murmured words and prayed for a while. Finally, he said: "This is a more ominous sign than the first one!"

Old King Nor-chen was greatly shocked and quickly asked, "What kind of ill omen? Great lama, pray tell me the truth!" The sorcerer He-ra said: "The oracle says explicitly that a disaster is near. If it is a minor one, the king will die; if it is a severe one, the country will fall into ruin and people all over the land will suffer."

The king asked the sorcerer to try to avert the disaster by prayer. But the sorcerer purposely pretended that it would be difficult to do so, and offered to do whatever was within his ability, saying to the king: "This is an extraordinary case. It is necessary to prepare special offerings to worship the deities. Prepare 120 khals of tsam-ba (roasted highland barley meal), 30 khals of highland barley, ten fat sheep, and ten loads of butter, as well as cloth of five colors, streamers, flags, ox hide, bows and arrows, and iron tripods. Also, the heart and liver of a semi-deity are especially needed."

The king said: "All the other offerings can be got ready at once, but where can I find the heart and liver of a semi-deity?"

The sorcerer said: "As for this, it is Your Majesty's great luck and the country's good fortune that we have Yid-vphrog-lha-mo, the daughter of a celestial musician! Isn't she a semi-deity? If we take her heart and liver as an offering to the gods, this will surely turn ill luck into good and danger into safety."

Old King Nor-chen said: "Ah ya! Yid-vphrog-lha-mo is the most beloved princess in my son Nor-bzang's heart. If her life is forfeited, how am I going to tell my son when he returns from fighting far away?

Pray think over this question again and see if we can use something else instead of the heart and liver of a semi-deity."

The sorcerer He-ra said: "Let's consider. The danger which is imminent will involve the loss of your life and that of Prince Nor-bzang, not to mention Yid-vphrog-lha-mo. By that time it would be too late to regret what you have done." Seeing that the prediction was so serious, the king entrusted the sorcerer and the 500 imperial concubines to take care of this affair.

The sorcerer accepted his order and led a contingent of troops and the 500 imperial concubines to encircle Yid-vphrog-lha-mo's dwelling as closely as possible. She did not know what was going on, so she asked the mother queen to go with her to the roof terrace to watch the scene.

There they saw the concubines and the sorcerer He-ra clamoring:

A net has been spread on the hilltop,

Where can the little eagle escape?

A trap has been set on the meadow,

Where can the little deer escape?

A device has been prepared in willow woods,

Where can the lark fly?

Troops have been deployed outside the palace,

Where can Yid-vphrog-lha-mo flee?

Hearing this, the mother queen and Yid-vphrog-lha-mo were very astonished. The mother queen advised the crowd below again and again not to act wildly. But the crowd spoke in one voice, saying that they acted upon the king's order to capture Yid-vphrog-lha-mo and open her chest to take out the heart. Yid-vphrog-lha-mo was terribly frightened and did not know what to do.

The mother queen said: "At his departure, Nor-bzang handed me a necklace, telling me that only when your life was in danger should I give it to you. I am afraid that now is the time."

Yid-vphrog-lha-mo took the necklace and, removing half the pearls, gave them to the queen, saying: "When Prince Nor-bzang comes back, he will certainly be grieved. Mother, pray give him these pearls. When he sees them, it will seem as though he had seen me." Then she put on the half string of pearls and through its power, soared into the air. Circling over the roof, she said:

A net has been spread on the hilltop,
Little eagle is unwilling to stay any longer,
It will fly to the high peak,
    to clean its feathers and gaze at blue sky.
An iron hook is put at the bottom of the lake,
Little fish is unwilling to stay any longer,
It will swim to the great sea,
    to drink a few mouthfuls of delicious water,
    to enrich its experience of the world.
A trap has been set on the meadow,
Little deer is unwilling to stay any longer,
It will run up to the snow mountain,
    to eat a few mouthfuls of tender grass,
    to flaunt its beautiful antlers.
A cage has been set in the willow woods,
The lark is unwilling to stay any longer,
It will fly to the birch woods,
    to meet some friends,
    to sing with its own melodious voice.
Farewell, dear friends,

Adieu! I cannot let your wish be fulfilled,
I am really sorry.

She circled in the sky for a while and then, without looking back, flew straight westward.

The sorcerer He-ra and the 500 imperial concubines were so amazed that they stared into the sky. The troops behind them were terrified and did not know what to do.

Yid-vphrog-lha-mo was deeply in love with the prince and did not wish to part with him without expressing her feelings. First she flew to the Ga-vu-ri-khrod Mountain cave beside the lake and found the old hermit. She told him of her frightening experience and said that Prince Nor-bzang would certainly come to look for her. "If he comes here, pray give him this jadeite ring and tell him how to get to my native place. Pray never forget." Then she flew back to her own home.

Meanwhile, Prince Nor-bzang led his troops through wind, snow and sands, advancing towards the northern wilderness. Despite countless hardships, he thought of the responsibility entrusted him by the people and the hope of returning home, and finally arrived outside the city of the enemy, where he made camp. There he inspected the terrain and made ready for the offensive.

As soon as the king of the enemy's country saw the mighty contingent of troops that had come to his territory, he realized it would be impossible to fight against them and so surrendered to Prince Nor-bzang. The prince made arrangements to deal with problems of the situation and immediately began the return with his troops to his own country.

When he had been advancing towards the savages' country, he had not felt the journey long, but now, on his way home, he always thought his horse ran too slowly. Crossing mountains and rivers, one after another, his horse galloped without stopping and forests seemed to be flying the other direction. But this did not ease his anxiety and eagerness to return. How Nor-bzang wished that he could become a bird and fly back to his palace!

The days passed one after another. Nor-bzang could no longer bear the lonely, monotonous pace, and, with a few cavaliers, hurried on to the capital. He ordered his troops to follow and catch up with him later.

When Prince Nor-bzang came to the top of Tiger Hill, a crow flew in his face and cawed three times overhead. Nor-bzang thought: "Alas! This crow must surely be the transformation of the mountain god. Perhaps some unfortunate event has happened in our palace!" So he dismounted and bowed down to pay homage with this prayer:

"Miraculous magic bird, pray listen to my prayer. Has some unfortunate event happened in the palace? Is it possible that my father, the king, is ill? If he is in good health, pray fly from left to right in three circles. If he is ill, pray fly from right to left in three circles."

The crow circled from left to right three times, and Nor-bzang knew that all was well with the king. Again he bowed and prayed:

"Miraculous magic bird, please listen to my prayer. Is it possible that my mother, the queen, is ill? If she is in good health, pray fly from left to right in three circles. If she is seriously ill, fly from right to left in three circles."

The crow again circled from left to right three times, and Nor-bzang knew his mother was in good health. Then he hesitated. Could some unfortunate event have happened to his beloved fairy maiden Yid-vphrog-lha-mo? Again he made his obeisance while silently saying a prayer:

"Miraculous magic bird, is it possible that some accident has happened to my beloved fairy maiden, my beautiful, gentle, wise, kind-hearted Yid-vphrog-lha-mo? If she is safe and sound in the palace, pray circle from left to right three times. If something unfortunate has befallen her, pray circle from right to left three times."

Strangely, the crow circled from right to left precisely three times, and Nor-bzang knew that something had befallen Yid-vphrog-lha-mo. He felt fire raging in his heart. He quickly wrote a letter, fastened it to the foot of the crow and asked the bird to carry it on ahead.

At this time, old King Nor-chen knew that Yid-vphrog-lha-mo had been forced to go away. He felt very sad and went for a walk in the palace. Suddenly, he saw a crow fly near him and drop a letter at his feet. It was the letter from Nor-bzang. The king was very glad to know that Nor-bzang had arrived at the Tiger Hill and was not far from the capital. The queen and the 500 imperial concubines heard that a letter had come from Nor-bzang and came to extend greetings. The king suddenly recalled what had happened to Yid-vphrog-lha-mo, so he gave them instructions: "When Nor-bzang comes back, you will all go to greet him. If he asks about Yid-vphrog-lha-mo, just say that she has gone back to the celestial musician's heavenly palace to visit her parents. Don't say anything else or you will be severely punished!"

When Nor-bzang reached the outskirts of the capital, a messenger came with the speed of shooting stars to report the news. People in the palace bustled about. The queen, leading the 500 imperial concubines, went out to welcome him. Seeing his mother, Nor-bzang was so happy that he could not help shedding tears. The queen asked him to stand on a woolen carpet and handed him a cup of wine. But Nor-bzang hesitated, and said: "Mother, you have given birth to me, nurtured me and reared me. Nobody in the world has lavished on me so much kindness. Thank you for such good wine and a kind reception. But why haven't I seen that person? Where is she? Why hasn't she come to welcome me?"

The queen found it difficult to answer. Tears filled her eyes. All the imperial concubines tried to put in a word, saying that Yid-vphrog-lha-mo found it hard to bear the loneliness and went to the heavenly palace to visit her parents. The queen was mute. Nor-bzang forced himself to finish a cup of wine but suspicion grew in his mind.

King Nor-chen and his officials stood at the palace entrance to welcome the hero. Nor-bzang approached and bowed to his father, the king, as usual and asked at once: "Honorable king, my father, where is my beloved Princess Yid-vphrog-lha-mo?"

Nonchalantly, the king said, "Oh, her! She has gone to the heavenly palace to visit he parents!"

Nor-bzang asked, "When will she come back?"

The king said, "Never mind! It makes no difference whether she comes back or not. I have 500 imperial concubines for you. If you still remember them, my mind will be at ease."

Nor-bzang said, "The 500 imperial concubines put together would not match Yid-vphrog-lha-mo."

"If you dislike the 500 imperial concubines and think them ugly, I can search for beautiful women in five directions and ten kingdoms across the land for your sake," said the king.

But Nor-bzang said, "No matter how beautiful a woman is, even as beautiful as a flower, a piece of jade or a peacock, I still want my Yid-vphrog-lha-mo. Wherever she is, even at the remotest corner of the earth, I will certainly find her. I hope you understand that."

Seeing that Prince Nor-bzang was so willful and stubborn, the king immediately became downcast, saying, "Can it be that the 500 imperial concubines cannot match Yid-vphrog-lha-mo? Can it be that beautiful women from across the land cannot match Yid-vphrog-lha-mo? Can it be that our country's magnificent landscape cannot match Yid-vphrog-lha-mo? If you insist on going in search of her, well, be gone at once. I don't want to see you anymore!"

Nor-bzang silently took off his war robe, helmet and armor and threw off the knife from his belt, preparing to leave.

The queen tried to persuade him to stay, brought him back to the palace and advised him not to be impatient. He stayed in the palace while his mother gave him a detailed account of what had happened to Yid-vphrog-lha-mo and the half string of pearls.

Three days passed. It was the fifteenth day of the fourth month again. When the moon rose from the eastern hill, Nor-bzang left the palace alone and walked quietly along the river, climbed the hilltop and gazed at a vast expanse of mist. He thought: "Yid-vphrog-lha-mo! Flower in my heart, where can I find you?" Then he turned over in his mind: "Yid-vphrog-lha-mo came to me through the guidance of the hermit in the Ga-vu-ri-khrod Mountain cave. As he was able to know that she and I were predestined for marriage, he would surely know her whereabouts. I will go and find him!" So he traveled all the way to the mountain cave.

In the Ga-vu-ri-khrod Mountain cave Prince Nor-bzang knelt in front of the hermit Blo-gros-rig-gsal's seat.

"Great lama, who knows the future and the past, pray protect me, a person who has been tortured. I feel like a blind man who has fallen into an abyss. Pray show me the way out! Pray tell me where Yid-vphrog-lha-mo has gone!" The hermit took out the ring which Yid-vphrog-lha-mo had left with him, gave it to Nor-bzang, and told him the way leading to the celestial musician's heavenly palace. He

55

also prayed for Nor-bzang's safe arrival at the heavenly palace and success in finding the fairy maiden.

Prince Nor-bzang put the beautiful ring tightly on his finger, memorized the route indicated by the hermit and set out with long strides.

First he came to the bank of the beautiful lake where Yid-vphrog-lha-mo had bathed. Nor-bzang himself took a bath there. After bathing he was imbued with infinite courage and high spirits. He continued to go on, day after day and night after night. He came to a mountain valley where he could see neither the sky nor the sun. Mosquitoes as big as sparrows filled the air, and flew over to bite him. Hurriedly recalling Yid-vphrog-lha-mo's words, the prince raised his hand with the ring on it, waving it to the left three times and to the right three times. The mosquitoes retreated one by one, making way for him.

Nor-bzang continued to go on, crossing hills and ridges, one after another, until he saw a white pagoda in the distance. He drew near the pagoda and circled round it to the right several times and bowed his obeisance. Then he went on. The stars were chasing the moon and the moon was chasing the sun.

When the prince came near a hill, he saw a square piece of crystal radiant with a sparkling light. A white *hata* (according to Tibetan custom a scarf presented to a person as a token of respect) was placed on the crystal. Nor-bzang took up the white *hata*, tied it around his neck and went on over a broad road linked to a small road and mountain paths linked to a plain. He came to a blue-gray stone slab in the shape of a reclining ox, with a gold seal beside it.

Following the hermit's instructions, Nor-bzang gripped the gold seal and rapped the horn of the stone ox with it several times. A fountain flowed out of the mouth of the stone ox. After drinking from the fountain, Nor-bzang forgot hunger and thirst and continued on his way. He crossed streams and rivers, one after another, and came to a dark, dense forest where tigers and lions roared, monkeys cried and wolves howled, making such a din. Nor-bzang hurriedly raised the ring on his hand and the wild beasts submissively sat at one side to make way for him. He crossed the forest and continued on his way. He could not remember how many days and nights he had walked.

At long last, he arrived at a flower garden where a hundred flowers were in bloom, spreading their fragrance everywhere. Nor-bzang was not in the leisurely mood to appreciate the beauty and aroma of the flowers. A four-forked road lay in front of him. He wondered which road would lead to the heavenly palace. As he hesitated, he waved the ring on his hand. He noticed a turquoise-colored wasp flying over his head, buzzing, buzzing, buzzing. So that was the guide! Nor-bzang flew in its wake. The wasp led Nor-bzang to a mountain peak with steep cliffs. Below, the mountain was seething with filthy water and thousands of poisonous snakes. Nor-bzang could not move one step. Suddenly a little deer ran towards him, and Nor-bzang knew that it would be his guide. Following the little deer, he went down the mountain, entered a valley and walked onto a plain and a grassland. He walked and walked. He continued on his way to the heavenly palace and walked to the large mountain peak that links up with the sky. He stood on the peak and, shading his eyes with his hands, looked in all directions.

Ah, he thought, that densely populated, bustling place—isn't it the celestial musician's heavenly palace? Nor-bzang's heart was pounding like the little deer. He felt as if his eyes were draped with a layer of white mist and his face burning with fire. He knew that he had arrived, at long last.

Nor-bzang came to a well and saw three maidens drawing water from it. He gently called to them, intending to make an inquiry. But the maidens were so frightened at the sight of a stranger that they threw down their buckets and ran and did not stop until they were quite far away. Then they turned and gazed at him. A very charming maiden asked, "Where do you come from, stranger? What has brought you to our native place?"

Nor-bzang said with a smile, "I have come from a faraway place to look for my beloved maiden. What is the name of this place? Why are you drawing water?"

The maidens said, "This is the heavenly palace, a marvelous, beautiful spot. No stranger has ever come here. As our elder sister Yid-vphrog-lha-mo has returned from the earthly world to heaven, we fetch water for her bath, to wash off the vulgar dust of the earthly world."

Hearing these words, Nor-bzang rejoiced. He took up the buckets from beside the well and stealthily dropped the ring into one of them. He said to the maidens, "To wash off the vulgar dust of the earthly world, it is necessary to bathe with all the water, splashing water downward to clean the whole body." The three maidens timidly took the buckets and ran home at full speed. They told Yid-vphrog-lha-mo that they had met a young man beside the well. She did not take any notice of this, thinking that her little sisters were making it up.

When the princess lifted up a bucket of water to bathe her body, she suddenly tipped the ring out of the bucket. Gazing at it carefully, she saw that it was the very same ring she had left for Nor-bzang. Only then did she believe her sisters had told the truth. She was both joyful and sad, anxious and agitated, happy and grieved, and fainted away. This frightened her youngest sister so much that she hurriedly ran to report to their father.

As soon as the king of celestial musicians, Rta-mgo-can, heard of this, he hurried to Yid-vphrog-lha-mo's side and helped to revive her. When she regained consciousness, she immediately asked her father, the king, to bring Nor-bzang to her. Only then did Rta-mgo-can know that Nor-bzang had come to the heavenly palace. He had no intention of permitting Yid-vphrog-lha-mo to meet with a mortal, but she wept and wailed, demanding to see him. She said Nor-bzang had saved her life. Moreover, he had left great wealth and high position in the world and crossed mountains on his long journey to the heavenly palace. She said she could not refuse to see him.

Rta-mgo-can became helpless and consented to allow the maiden and the prince to talk to each other, but only with a curtain between them, not face-to-face.

When Yid-vphrog-lha-mo saw Nor-bzang draw near, she became dizzy. At the sight of Yid-vphrog-lha-mo, Nor-bzang swept the curtain away and the lovers held each other in a warm embrace. Yid-vphrog-lha-mo was speechless. They could not tell whose tears were streaming down their cheeks. They were murmuring words and could not tell who was saying them. At long last they were together.

When Nor-bzang paid homage to Rta-mgo-can, the king of celestial musicians could hardly remain in his seat. Nor-bzang spoke of his intention to take Yid-vphrog-lha-mo back to the earthly world to enjoy happiness, but her father had no intention of permitting it. Rta-mgo-can talked evasively and thought of various pretexts to prevent it. Finally, he said, "Many princes in our heavenly palace wished to marry Yid-vphrog-lha-mo, and if you took her away, it would cause disputes. It would be best for all of you to take part in a contest of martial skills. Whoever excels in the contest is entitled to marry and take away Yid-vphrog-lha-mo."

Nor-bzang consented to the celestial king's requirement.

Rta-mgo-can dressed up his four most talented and resourceful ministers as if they were princes who had come from other countries as suitors. They went with Nor-bzang to the grounds outside the eastern gate to compete in archery. The drill ground was surrounded with spectators. The four false princes each shot an arrow through a white poplar tree. Swollen with pride, they thought to themselves that they were wonderful.

Unexpectedly, Prince Nor-bzang pulled his bow taut and shot; one arrow shot through three white poplars and three stone oxen. The spectators were stupefied. King Rta-mgo-can could not utter a word, but was still reluctant to let Yid-vphrog-lha-mo leave for the earthly world to live with Nor-bzang. He could do nothing but evade Nor-bzang's request with an excuse. Nor-bzang insisted that the promise must be kept. Then Yid-vphrog-lha-mo's mother stepped forward with a suggestion: "Depending on this contest alone, I am afraid, would not convince everybody. Tomorrow let us gather all the maidens in the land, with Yid-vphrog-lha-mo among them. You, the five princes, will shoot arrows on the square in front of the palace. Whoever your arrow falls upon will become your wife. Whoever's arrow falls on Yid-vphrog-lha-mo, she will become your wife."

The next day, everybody gathered on the palace square. The four false princes shot their arrows into the sky and none of them fell on Yid-vphrog-lha-mo. After Nor-bzang's arrow had been shot into the sky, it whirled there as if it had wings and finally fell straight onto Yid-vphrog-lha-mo's bosom without slanting at all. She was overjoyed and the prince was extremely happy, but the king was sad and all the crowd was shocked. King Rta-mgo-can decided to send Yid-vphrog-lha-mo and Nor-bzang back to the earthly world. He gave a wealth of gold, silver and jewelry, camels, horses, silks, gauzes, satins and brocades as her dowry. He escorted them right to the lake and only then did he part from them.

Nor-bzang took Yid-vphrog-lha-mo back again into his palace. Old King Nor-chen had mixed feelings of grief, shame and happiness. Later, Nor-chen gave banquets for seven days and nights to celebrate their peaceful return. The palace was as lively and bustling inside and out as the heavenly palace. Those 500 imperial concubines and the sorcerer He-ra received the punishment they deserved.

A short time afterward, the old king passed the throne to Nor-bzang, and Yid-vphrog-lha-mo became queen. From then on, the people of the northern country Sngags-ldan-pa led a happier, more satisfied and more pleasant life than they had ever known before.

MAIDEN VGRO-BA-BZANG-MO

The play was adapted from the Tibetan folk story "Elder Sister and Brother;" even today it circulates in the form of a ballad among the people. The titles of most of the other operas based on this tale have used the name of the heroine of this opera.

In the old days, a king named Ka-la-dbang-po ruled in Mandra Sgang. His queen's name was Ha-cang-bdud-mo, whose name means "terrible devilish woman." She was a female demon and had given birth to neither boy nor girl. Her heart was more savage than a wolf and more venomous than a snake.

One day, King Ka-la-dbang-po hoisted a large banner over the roof of his palace, blew the largest conch towards the sky, beat the largest drum on the terrace of the roof and brought together all the ministers and common people to the public square outside the palace. Then King Ka-la-dbang-po spoke to the ministers and the people: "Ministers! Commoners! Please listen to me! Day after tomorrow when the sun is shining over the palace, we will go hunting at the top of the mountain in the east. Whoever has bows and arrows at home, bring them along, and those who have no bows and arrows can take them from my armory. Everybody must get ready at once to set off for the hunt."

A minister named Tri-nan-vdzin came forward, saying to the king: "Noble King, pray listen to what I say. In my humble opinion, you had better not go hunting. When a king goes out hunting and kills

living creatures, he can expect to be ridiculed by people of neighboring countries. Even when a commoner goes out hunting, he is looked
down upon by others. You had better not go out hunting."

The king disagreed with what the minister had said. He remarked:
"Listen to me, once and for all. A king's words are like stones rolling
down the cliffs. The stones can never roll upward. A king's words
sound like flowing water in a river, and can never flow upward. Even
if your advice were most valuable, you must first look around at the
neighboring countries. Which of these countries has its own treasures?
What's are my treasures except the hunting dog Rgya-khra-ba-shi?
What's the use of a precious hunting dog if I don't go out hunting?
What kind of a treasure is that? You had better close your mouth and
get ready to set out!"

On the morning of the third day, when the sun was shining over the
palace, all the ministers and commoners were outfitted with firearms
and bows and arrows, and were clad like hunters. Leading the hunting
dog, the king set out up the hill at the head of all others.

They traveled over the tops of all the mountains in the east but
failed to capture any wild beast. Later, near the border of their land,
they climbed a high mountain and caught thirty-seven David's deer.
But the precious hound, Rgya-khra-ba-shi, disappeared that night like
a rainbow on the sky. Nobody knew where he had gone. The king was
terribly worried and said to the ministers and commoners: "Ministers!
Commoners! Today we have traveled with the sun for one day but
my Rgya-khra-ba-shi is lost. You know the dog is my indispensable
treasure. I would rather die than go back without finding it. Let us
sleep here in the open air tonight. As soon as the sun rises, we will all
go in search of Rgya-khra-ba-shi!"

The king, the ministers and all commoners slept with the rifles and bows and arrows as their pillows, under the starlight throughout the night.

The next day as soon as it dawned, the king woke up minister Tri-nan-vdzin, saying: "Get up! Get up! Look around and listen carefully for sounds of people shouting and dogs barking. Search for footprints of the hound!"

The minister Tri-nan-vdzin got up, listened carefully and looked around in all directions. He did not see any footprints of the hound or hear its barking. He felt very gloomy and, climbing up a large mountain, looked around once again. He saw a dense forest in the east with a flatland in its heart, and a small house in the center of the flatland. The small house was typical of the region, and smoke was rising from the kitchen chimney. Tri-nan-vdzin wondered: "Maybe the dog has gone there? So he hurried back to the king and reported to him: "Honorable King, I acted upon your order to search for the hunting dog Rgya-khra-ba-shi. All the way I heard no people shouting or dogs barking and saw no dog's footprints. I was almost certain the hound was lost. Later, I climbed up a big mountain and looked. Well, in a large forest in the east there was a small flatland on which stood a small house, and smoke was rising from its kitchen chimney. Certainly, it is a place where people are living. That hound Rgya-khra-ba-shi most probably has gone there."

When the king heard Tri-nan-vdzin's story, he was overjoyed and said to him: "You are indeed the flower of my heart, and really a sage of Buddhist logic, Sanskrit, arts and crafts and medicine. That hound Rgya-khra-ba-shi must be there. Let's go! Let's go in search of it!"

King Ka-la-dbang-po marched at the head of all the ministers and commoners until they came right up to the small house on the flatland in the forest. Just as they expected, they found something just like the dog's footprints. The minister Tri-nan-vdzin went up to knock at the gate. A moment later, a hermit appeared at the drainage trough on the roof. His hair was as white as a conch, his eyes as blue as turquoise and he had not a single tooth in his mouth, not even one the size of a small pearl. He could stand only by leaning on a staff. He asked the people below: "Who are you?"

The king took a propitious *hata*, a silk scarf presented as a sign of respect, from his own metal amulet box and hung it on the tip of a bamboo pole, saying: "Elderly hermit, please listen to me. We have all come from Mandra Sgang. My name is Ka-la-dbang-po. Yesterday morning, we came out hunting for our own amusement, and caught thirty-seven David's deer. In the afternoon, at dusk, we lost a hound. This morning, our search for the hound led us here and we discovered the dog's footprints at your door. Please return the hound to me right away!"

When the old hermit heard this, he was shocked, and he said to himself, "Ka-la-dbang-po's law is strict and his power very strong, even more burning than flames, more turbulent than sea waves, sharper than the tip of a needle and finer than the hair of a horse's tail. I had heard of him but I have never seen his countenance. He would not condescend to come to my place except of necessity." Thinking this, he trembled and tottered to open the door, and knelt down on the ground.

With his palms pressed together, he said to the king:

"Honorable King! My wife and I are so old that we nearly have to crawl along when we are walking. Since our early days we have never been glib talkers. Now we have nothing but old bones and one foot in the grave; we are even less able to speak well. We don't know that you have a hunting dog and we've never seen one. Even if we had seen it, it would be of no use to us. Your Majesty, if you don't believe my words, pray come into the house to search for it!"

The king, the ministers and the attendants rushed into the house and searched everywhere for the dog but they found nothing. All they saw in the room with three doors was the hermit's old wife. Her hair was also as white as a conch and her eyes as blue as turquoise. In her mouth there was not a single tooth, even one the size of a small pearl. She could stand up only by leaning on a staff. She was counting a string of prayer beads.

The king thought to himself:

"These are two hermits of such longevity and with so many possessions, maybe the God of Mercy is protecting them!" With this thought, reverence for the Buddha sprang up in his mind. But even so, his eagerness to search for the dog and his worry and anxiety urged him to search every corner. Finding a room with the door locked, he said to the hermit's wife: "Be quick! Open this door and let me look in this room. Perhaps my hound is hidden inside."

"Honorable King," said the hermit, "my wife and I are so old that we almost have to crawl when we walk. Since our early days we have not been glib talkers. Now we have nothing but old bones left and one foot in the grave. We become less able to speak well, We've neither seen nor known your hunting dog. Your Majesty, if you don't believe us, we can open this room. But pray do not put forward any unreasonable demand!"

The door of the room was opened. When the king entered, he saw a maiden who certainly was not of the ordinary world, but a fairy from heaven. Wearing a pure white costume and with a white, soft complexion, she had the enchanting features of a goddess. She was sparkling in the eye, pleasant to the ear and had a sweet, delicious breath.

As soon as the king saw her, he lost his heart. He thought: "My hound Rgya-khra-ba-shi disappeared without any reason. The dog's footprints happened to be found just in front of the hermit's door. Perhaps heaven is directing me here!" He took out a beautiful turquoise hairpin and placed it in the hair of the beautiful maiden.

Turning, he said to the hermit: "You must give your daughter in marriage to me. From this moment on, don't try to pretend that the maiden has flown up to heaven or plunged into the ground, been taken away by force by a family of great importance, or bought by a wealthy family, stolen by a robber or thief or taken to wife by an insignificant family. If you dare to say any of these things, watch out for your old life! Day after tomorrow when the sun rises, I will send somebody to bring her to my place. No matter how much money you demand or how many slaves you want, I will satisfy your demand. But you must get ready to send her to me."

With these words, the king went back to Mandra Sgang, leading his ministers and commoners.

Meanwhile, after King Ka-la-dbang-po had gone, the fairy Vgro-ba-bzang-mo thought to herself: "Why should I become the wife of a tyrant who has committed heinous crimes? I would be better off dead. I remember my mother saying that the fifth goddess advised that if I face any tribulation, I should fly up to the sky. I think that this must be a tribulation! Really I should depart."

So Vgro-ba-bzang-mo made up her mind and, spreading the hem of her dress as wings, she intended to fly up to heaven. At that moment, the old hermit and his wife saw what she was going to do and the old father tottered to her side, grasped her gown and said, "My good daughter Vgro-ba-bzang-mo, listen to your father. If you fly away and

67

leave us behind, you know that the stern king of Mandra Sgang will punish us with death. Good child! Think of the old people! Don't fly away, listen to my words!" With these words, tears welled up in his eyes like spring water.

The old woman also came tremblingly forward and grasped the other side of Vgro-ba-bzang-mo's gown. "How strange you are, my maiden," she said. "When you were born, the fifth goddess instructed that if you met tribulation, you should fly up to the sky. But this does not mean that you should fly up to heaven at the first tribulation you meet. You were advised to fly up to heaven on the third occasion, that is, the last tribulation. Now, this is the first tribulation you've met and it is not yet time for you to fly up. Good maiden, think carefully!" With these words, the old lady also shed many tears.

Vgro-ba-bzang-mo thought over these things. "Alas!" she thought. "My father and mother deserve pity. I cannot set my mind at ease about them. Can I find a way out?" She could only wipe away the tears streaming down her cheeks. But somehow she obeyed her parents and went back to her room. The old couple now were at ease in their minds.

On the morning of the third day, the king, the ministers and the commoners from Mandra Sgang came riding on horses, elephants and camels laden with all sorts of treasures, including jewels, gold, silver, gowns and precious objects beyond anyone's imagination. They came to welcome and take Vgro-ba-bzang-mo back with them as a bride. The old couple hurriedly dressed her in elaborate clothing.

The maiden Vgro-ba-bzang-mo rode a swift black steed with four white legs, the king a sturdy light yellow horse, minister Tri-nan-vdzin on a gelding and all the others followed in procession, returning to the palace accompanied by a mighty army of drummers and musicians.

The common folk of Mandra Sgang from near and far prepared a solemn ceremony to welcome them.

When the procession reached the palace, the king sat on a block of gold and Vgro-ba-bzang-mo on a block of jade. The rays of the golden block and the jade block shone on each other and all over the palace, and the transparency and brilliance of the palace was like the ideal fairyland of the Buddhists.

There was a great banquet in the palace. Afterward, Vgro-ba-bzang-mo said to the king: "No matter how much happiness and wealth we enjoy in this world, they will vanish like a dream in the spring. Your Majesty! You had better become a devotee of Buddhism."

Because her words satisfied the king, he ordered flags hoisted over the palace, conches blown, and drums beaten. The commoners gathered. The king addressed them: "Ministers and commoners, my hunting dog Rgya-khra-ba-shi got lost and his footprints were found at the door of a hermit's house. All of you are aware of this. Very probably this is Vgro-ba-bzang-mo's supernatural power. She is a Great Master devoted to Buddhist teachings. Beginning this day, I am a devotee of Buddhism. All of you should follow my example and believe in the Buddhist teachings...."

From then on, people of Mandra Sgang led a happier life than before. Indeed, it was prosperous, auspicious and satisfactory. Their hopes and dreams came true.

Later, Vgro-ba-bzang-mo lived in an extremely quiet place in the palace and practiced Buddhist meditation. Several months afterward, she gave birth to a princess named Kun-tu-bzang-mo and three years later, a prince named Kun-tu-legs-pa. The mother, the children and the king all were extraordinarily happy. One day, the king sang the following lines to Vgro-ba-bzang-mo:

My flower-like beloved queen!
Pray listen to what I say:
I have seen through everything in the world,
That's why I revere and love Buddhist teachings.
I shall sit quietly in meditation,
   according to ascetic Buddhist rules,
   in a mountain cave.
Let us put all our clothing and food in one room,
   to be used freely by our children—elder sister
   and younger brother.
Respected and beloved Vgro-ba-bzang-mo,
As you have already borne a daughter and a son,
You may set your mind at ease and quietly practice Buddhism.
My flower Vgro-ba-bzang-mo!

After listening to King Ka-la-dbang-po's song, Vgro-ba-bzang-mo
sang in reply:
My venerable, widely influential king!
Pray listen to what I shall say,
I cannot live with my parents in freedom,
   like tethered cattle and horses,
   or like a cow led away from a herd of cattle.
This place at the top of a snow mountain
   has suffering of heat and cold,
I shall undergo all sorts of tribulations!
Your Majesty, you leave us behind to practice
   rigorous Buddhism.
We envy you,

It's far better than receiving homage of officials
   and commoners.
No matter how well-fed and well-dressed you are,
Everything vanishes at your death.
Neither mountain nor stream can shelter you.
When tribulations come upon me,
I shall also fly up to heaven!

Then the king and queen went separately to their rooms to sit in closed-door meditation for several years.

Ha-cang-bdud-mo, the queen whom the king had married earlier, had a trusted maidservant named Ze-ma-ra-mgo (meaning "a shrew"). One day, when this maidservant went to the roof of the palace, she spied Vgro-ba-bzang-mo and her two children. She murmured to herself:

"What a shame for Ha-cang-bdud-mo! The king has a new queen who has borne a prince to inherit the throne and a princess to establish marriage ties. But we are kept in the dark!" She sped off to Ha-cang-bdud-mo and told her what she had seen. Ha-cang-bdud-mo pondered: "Ze-ma-ra-mgo's words can usually be trusted." So she went up to the roof and carefully looked around. When she looked at the building where Vgro-ba-bzang-mo sat in meditation, she saw her and the two children. Jealousy flamed up in her heart and her face became blue with anger. She cursed: "My name is Ha-cang-bdud-mo and I am the sworn enemy of you and your children! If I don't eat up the three of you today, may our guardian gods come and eat me!" She took an oath, gnashed her long, sharp, protruding teeth three times with a crunching sound, and then went back to her room.

Vgro-ba-bzang-mo saw all these things and thought: "Long ago,

71

the goddess predicted that I would suffer the torment of demons. Perhaps she meant this female demon. When will be the proper time if I don't go away now?"

At once she sent the prince to the king and clasped in her arms the princess, who looked like a blossoming lotus flower. With tears running down her face, the queen sobbed: "My good daughter, my darling. When your mama was born, the goddess predicted she would be tormented by a female demon. Now this female demon Ha-cang-bdud-mo is going to persecute us. If I stay on here, we three will die together and be buried in her belly. Come on, my dear child, let mama put ornaments on you. Ask your father the king to take good care of you and your brother's life and prospects. Mama cannot linger here and must fly to the place where the goddess lives in fairyland."

With these words, tears rolled down her cheeks like pearls from a broken string. She took off her ornaments and clothing and put them on her daughter. Then she flew up to heaven like a gust of wind.

The princess wanted to fly off with her mother, but after having flown only about ten feet, dropped to the ground. She went back to her mother's room, weeping. That room looked like a nest whose birds have flown away. It was full of desolation and loneliness. The princess felt much distressed, as if she were drunk, stunned, in a trance and dying.

When Prince Kun-tu-legs-pa returned from his father the king, he walked into his mother's room but did not see her. He saw only his sister weeping so bitterly as to be nearly dead. He asked: "Where is our mama? My elder sister, why are you so grieved?" The princess said to him, "Our mama has flown up to heaven, leaving the two of us behind. Let's go to our father the king." Weeping, they told him how their mother had flown off.

When the king heard that Vgro-ba-bzang-mo had flown away, he was shocked and fell immediately into a coma. The ministers sprayed sandalwood water on his face, and only then did he regain consciousness. He said to all those present, with tears streaming down his face: "A popular saying goes: 'We can believe only half of a distant hearsay,' but this news does not come from far away. I myself must go and have a look." So he went to the palace where Vgro-ba-bzang-mo had lived. Pushing the door open and looking inside, he found the queen gone and the room empty, like a bird's nest with eggs stolen away. The king was very sorrowful and pulled his clothes over his head and wept bitterly.

The little prince threw himself into his father's arms and kissed his cheeks. He nestled close to the king, saying: "Papa, mama flew up to fairyland, just as if she died. It's no use for us to keep on grieving. We had better pray for her and ask her to come back soon to the palace."

The king thought: "This little prince of mine, although very young, knows how to comfort others. His words make good sense. He seems to be a reincarnation of the God of Compassion." Holding the little prince with his right hand and the princess with his left, the king walked up to the roof of Sgrol-ma-lha-khang and prayed:

"My dear Vgro-ba-bzang-mo, please listen to what we are going to say. Don't withdraw to fairyland all of a sudden, please come back to the palace." But not a single echo was heard from her. They were much distressed.

At that time, the female demon, Ha-cang-bdud-mo, called together all the ministers and said to them: "You all know that King Ka-la-dbang-po formerly vowed that he would never marry another queen. But he forgot what he had said and married Vgro-ba-bzang-mo. He has never come to see me for years. As you all know, many kings and princes in India have a number of wives, but they all live together. If Ka-la-dbang-po brought Vgro-ba-bzang-mo to live together with me, I wouldn't complain. But how can I tolerate the way he has behaved? Pray all of you give me some help. I will repay you any way you ask. Vgro-ba-bzang-mo has flown away but the children she left behind are still here. We must find ways to deal with that foolish King Ka-la-dbang-po."

After listening to Ha-cang-bdud-mo, several wicked ministers worked out a scheme to deceive the king. They got a bottle of medicinal solution that would make anyone who drank it insane. When they came into the king's presence, they said: "Your Majesty, although Vgro-ba-bzang-mo has flown up to heaven and resides there, you still have your beloved queen, a prince to inherit your throne and a princess to extend marriage ties. Don't grieve, pray drink some sweet wine to drive away your cares!"

The king did not suspect a trick, or that poison had been put in the bottle. He thought that these officials were kind and wanted to comfort him. So he drank one swallow after another until it was all gone. Soon he was out of his senses. He got up and he lay down over and over, shouting and clamoring for Vgro-ba-bzang-mo, staring into the distance. He sang and he danced. Seizing her chance, the female demon Ha-cang-bdud-mo said to all ministers and commoners, "The king has gone mad and cannot govern the affairs of state. We must shut him up in a dark dungeon at once!" The people could see that the king behaved very strangely and thought there was nothing else to do. This was how the female demon Ha-cang-bdud-mo usurped the rule of the country.

Then she thought: "If you do not put out flames when they are small, when they burn into a stack of straw as high as Mount Sumeru, there will be the danger of being burned by them; if you do not block a breach when it is small, a whole continent will be in danger of being flooded. If I do not get rid of the two small creatures left behind by Vgro-ba-bzang-mo, I will not be able to fight them when they grow up. If I order the ministers to kill them, they certainly will not agree to do so. I must think of another way."

A few days later, Ha-cang-bdud-mo feigned illness. She made a bed on the floor and underneath she put a piece of rotten ox hide. Then she smeared some stinking marrow on her body, some red earth on her right cheek and some indigo-blue on her left cheek. She lay on the bed, groaning aloud.

Hearing of her condition, the ministers thronged to Ha-cang-bdud-mo's bedside to inquire about her health: "How are you? What is your illness? Is there any pain? We'll pray to the deities or call in a doctor if you wish. What will do you some good?"

Ha-cang-bdud-mo said, groaning, "What's the use in praying to the deities? How can a doctor diagnose my illness? There is something—but I'm afraid you won't agree to carry it out!"

The ministers quickly assured her: "The prince and the princess are too young to shoulder the responsibilities of the state. You are the only one who can do it. Pray tell us whatever we can do to restore your health and we will certainly carry it out, by heaven!"

When Ha-cang-bdud-mo heard them take this oath, she said slowly, "No other method will work, there is only one miraculous cure: Take out the hearts of the prince and the princess. As soon as I eat them, I will certainly be cured. But you couldn't be expected to do such a thing!"

The ministers looked at one another and said, "There is no other way out. If this will restore your health, we'll certainly do it."

As soon as the ministers had agreed to do the deed, Ha-cang-bdud-mo said, "Well, be quick to fetch two butchers." So the ministers hurried to find two butchers and brought them to Ha-cang-bdud-mo's presence. She said to them: "Listen, you two! Kill the little prince and the princess and bring their hearts to me still warm. I'll give you any reward you would like to have."

The butchers accepted the order and went to where the prince and the princess lived.

The prince and the princess were young and carefree, but as soon as the prince saw the butchers, he was extremely frightened and said, "When you used to bring us meat, we were very glad to see you. But now I feel frightened when you come. Why is this? What are you coming for?" He thought for a moment. "Now all the ministers obey Ha-cang-bdud-mo. They sent you to kill us, didn't they?"

The butchers said nothing, and the prince continued: "What crime have my sister and I committed? What evil conduct? Don't you feel sorry? Pray think it over, both of you!" Tears streamed down his face like pearls.

Pity sprang up in the heart of the younger butcher. He said to his elder brother, the big butcher: "When Vgro-ba-bzang-mo was here, we did not even dare tread upon their shadows. How can we be so hard-hearted now as to kill them? I think we'd better let them go and kill the pair of little dogs behind the palace instead. We can give the dogs' hearts to be eaten by Ha-cang-bdud-mo. How about that, elder brother?"

The younger brother's words coincided with his own thoughts, so the big butcher said to the children, "Today, Ha-cang-bdud-mo and the ministers sent us to kill you. When Vgro-ba-bzang-mo was here, we did not even dare to tread on your shadows. How could we kill you today? After we leave, pray never play in the garden. If Ha-cang-bdud-mo got a glimpse of you, she would never spare your lives. Pray remember this."

The two butchers left, ran to the back entrance of the palace, killed the two dogs and took out their hearts. Then they went to Ha-cang-bdud-mo and said: "Honorable queen, the bigger one is Princess Kun-tu-bzang-mo's heart and the smaller one Kun-tu-legs-pa's heart. Please eat them up."

Pleased, Ha-cang-bdud-mo asked what reward the two butchers would like to have.

"We don't want any reward," they said, presenting her with the dogs' hearts, and went home.

Ha-cang-bdud-mo quickly dipped the dogs' hearts in salt and swallowed them in a few mouthfuls, believing they were human hearts. At once she wiped away the colors smeared on her face. Her illness was cured in a moment, and she was able to go to the roof of the palace for amusement every day.

But the prince and the princess were, after all, still children, and forgot the butchers' warnings in a few days. They went again to play in the garden and, as luck would have it, were again seen by Ha-cang-bdud-mo. She said with deep hatred, "Alas! It turns out that the two butchers haven't killed the two little beasts after all! There they are, still playing in the garden. I don't know what dirty things the butchers brought to hoodwink me. And look! The ministers love the two children as before."

So, just as she had done before, the female demon again set up a big bed and lay down on it, pretending to be ill. She took off her clothes and ornaments and put them beside her pillow. She moaned without stopping. "Ouch, ah!" The ministers once again rushed to her

77

bedside and asked: "How is your health? Has your illness relapsed? What shall we do to restore your health?" Ha-cang-bdud-mo did not say a word, but turned her face to the wall and slept. The ministers walked around the bed and pleaded: "King Ka-la-dbang-po is going mad. He's useless. Vgro-ba-bzang-mo flew up to heaven and the prince and the princess she left behind were killed by the butchers. There is no one in our hearts except you the queen. Without you, we really don't know what we would do."

Ha-cang-bdud-mo bade her attendants to prop her up, and scolded the ministers: "Peacocks have beautiful feathers but eat poisonous snakes. Your words are pleasant to the ear but your deeds are wicked. You told the two butchers to give me filthy things to eat and spared those two little beasts, the children. Now my illness is getting worse because of the filthy things I ate. If I fall ill, let it be so, if I am dying, let me die. This is no concern of yours." With these words she again lay down to sleep.

In their anxiety, the ministers bowed to her over and over, saying: "Although the prince would inherit the throne and the princess would develop marriage ties, we will overlook these things. We will surely try once again to take out their hearts to treat your illness."

Ha-cang-bdud-mo, making a long face, said: "Well, be quick to find two fishermen!"

The ministers immediately went out to find two fishermen and brought them to Ha-cang-bdud-mo's presence in the palace. She said to them: "You two fishermen, listen to my instructions. The younger of you must go and throw the prince into a lake. The older one must throw the princess into a lake. When you've done the job, I'll grant you a handsome reward."

Accepting her order, the two fishermen went to where the prince and the princess lived.

When they saw the two fishermen approaching, the children said, "When you used to come near us, we were very glad. Now when you come near, we feel extremely frightened. Ha-cang-bdud-mo has sent you to kill us, hasn't she? What crimes have we committed? Are you so hard-hearted as to kill us two innocents for no reason at all? Fishermen, brothers, pray think over this carefully."

The fishermen said, "Quite right! Ha-cang-bdud-mo and the ministers worked out a plan to order us to send you to the king of hell."

Hearing this, the prince said to his sister: "Because we did charitable and pious deeds in our previous incarnation, we were born as human beings. But now we have to die at the hands of the fishermen. Look at the tree beside the palace: The powerful eagle lives on the upper branches and the small sparrows live on the lower branches. Even birds show difference in rank. Alas! We would rather be the little sparrows beneath the eagle! All this happens because we no longer have our mother. Mama, we can only see you in dreams, pray come and take good care of my sister and me." Tears poured down his face like rain.

The two fishermen said: "Last time you two little fellows persuaded the butchers with sweet words to let you go. But we won't listen to that kind of thing from you!" Thereupon, they tied up the prince and his sister tightly, round after round, as if they were enemies. They led them out of the city. When they arrived at the city gates, all the people of the city thronged to look at them, and sighed: "It's a pity that a fresh flower is killed by frost before being offered to a holy place!" But the people were afraid because Ha-cang-bdud-mo was powerful and ruthless, and nobody dared to step forward to save the prince and his elder sister. The fishermen led them all the way to the seaside.

The prince said to the princess: "My sister, look at the geese in the lake. All ganders, the fathers, walk at the head of the group and female geese, the mothers, follow behind. How happy the little geese are, swimming in between and enjoying family happiness. Although we are prince and princess, we are far less happy than the young geese. Alas! Our mama whom we can only see in dreams, pray come and take care of me and my sister!" They wept so bitterly as to be all tears. But, even so, the fishermen stripped off all their clothes and ornaments.

When the younger fisherman was carrying the prince on his back to throw him into the lake, the prince said: "Now I'm going to die. Let me say three prayers before my death? The fisherman said, "You must not make malicious curses. You are only allowed to say well-meaning prayers."

The prince said: "Why should I make malicious curses? It's because I didn't do charitable deeds in my previous incarnation that I am doomed to such an end in this life." So he prayed for a while.

Hearing his prayers, the younger fisherman was moved and said to the elder fisherman: "When Vgro-ba-bzang-mo was here, we did not dare to tread upon their shadows, how can we kill them now? I think we'd better do a charitable deed and set them free. We ourselves needn't go back either. We'll go elsewhere to earn a living." The elder fisherman was also very moved. So they gave the children's clothes and ornaments back to them and advised them not to stay in Mandra Sgang any longer, but to flee for their lives to Sapurong, in the east.

The prince and the princess, like a pair of lambs in a deep mountain, did not know where to go. They had no choice but to go to Sapurong. They walked day after day. They entered a vast forest which they could not see through. They were hungry and thirsty and afraid of poisonous snakes. They had to eat some wild fruits and undergo all sorts of hardships. They walked towards Sapurong step by step.

Who would have thought that the vicious Ha-cang-bdud-mo would again see the figures of the prince and the princess from the roof of the palace? But she did, and sent the ministers on horseback to chase them. She ordered them to be tied up with ropes after they were captured, and she insisted that she would lead them back herself so that she could be sure they were caught. The ministers galloped off.

When they caught up with the children, the ministers said slyly, "The king has been set free from the dark dungeon and Vgro-ba-bzang-mo has returned from fairyland to the palace. They were anxiously searching for you two, their darlings. Stop at once, don't run off. Come back with us to the palace."

The prince and the princess believed their words and stopped. The ministers galloped up, seized them at once just like a wolf seizing sheep or an eagle seizing little birds. They carried the children straight back to Mandra Sgang.

When Ha-cang-bdud-mo saw them, anger sprang up in her heart. Gnashing her teeth, she scolded them: "Two little beasts! My name is Ha-cang. Today I'll teach you a lesson and you'll find out what a shrew I am." With these words, she imprisoned them in a dungeon without a drop of water to drink.

Early the next morning, she gave them to two hunters and ordered them to carry the children to the top of a mountain and throw them off to their death. The next day, two hunters did come and carry them to the Eastern Mountain in India. Seeing a herd of deer grazing there on a grassland, the prince said to the princess: "My sister! Look, the male deer, the father, walks in front and female deer, the mother, follows behind. The little deer are the young that roam leisurely in between.

81

Alas! Although we are prince and princess, we cannot enjoy family happiness like the young of the deer."

The hunters ignored their words. When the younger hunter was lifting up the prince, about to throw him off the mountain, the prince said to him: "Brave, vigorous hunter, please let me say my prayers to heaven before my death." With these words, he prayed as he had done the other times.

Carrying the princess on his back, the elder hunter heard these prayers and was much moved. He advised his younger brother: "Once, we didn't dare to tread upon their shadows. Now we are going to kill them. How can we be so hard-hearted? We'd better let them flee for their lives." The younger hunter said: "I don't care about good or evil. If you don't throw the princess, I will be glad to throw them both!"

But the elder hunter said, "If you won't let them flee for their lives, I myself shall deal with the princess, whom I am responsible for throwing off the mountain. You have no right to bother about my business." So he unfastened the ropes from the princess and allowed her to flee.

The younger hunter lifted the prince up and threw him right off a steep cliff. But Vgro-ba-bzang-mo, watching from above, changed herself into a huge eagle and with her wings brushed him away from the rocks and he fell into a lake. A parrot led him to the shore. The parrot said: "All our people of Padmacan are devotees of Buddhism, but in recent years the Buddhist inheritance was broken off. Pray come and rule as our king, won't you?"

The prince said, "Do you think I am qualified?" The parrot bowed towards all directions and the prince kowtowed with it and prayed, with palms pressed together. Immediately flown to him in the air were a light yellow robe, a sash studded with many gems, a pair of shoes and a scarf. The parrot helped decorate the prince and then flew to the presence of the Bram-ze deity, saying: "Hasn't the royal line of our kingdom of Padmacan been broken off for a long time? Now, under the sandalwood tree is a prince who is a deity come down from heaven. How nice it would be to ask him to be our king!"

When the deity heard this, he was so happy that he threw away his staff and, running to Padmacan, shouted: "Happiness comes to our people of Padmacan! Now a prince, a deity from heaven, is under the Tsandan tree. A parrot has flown to give us the message. Let us go quickly to ask him to be our king!"

He shouted so loud that all the commoners were startled. They hurriedly equipped a fine horse with a golden saddle and jade bridle, flew pennants and yellow parasols, beat drums and blew trumpets. With this grand display they welcomed the prince to the kingdom of Padmacan to take over the throne. Since that time, the people of this kingdom have been happier than ever before.

Now, after the elder hunter had set the princess free, he advised her to cross a large mountain to get to the kingdom of Padmacan and go from there to Sapurong. Sorrowfully, the princess rushed below the cliff to look for her brother's corpse, but in vain. She wandered towards Padmacan, shabbily dressed like a beggar.

Meanwhile, as king of Padmacan, the prince freely gave alms and honored the triad of the Buddha, the dharma, and the sangha. The princess went with other beggars into the palace to receive the alms. There she was recognized by the prince, and the sister and the brother were overjoyed to meet again. She stayed on in Padmacan to lead a life of happiness and security.

A short time afterward, news about their whereabouts reached Ha-cang-bdud-mo's ears. She blew a bigger trumpet than ever blown, beat a bigger drum than ever beaten and brought together all the ministers and commoners of the country. She said, "The two little beasts now are entrenched in the Padmacan kingdom. This is very unfavorable to us. Tomorrow morning, you will go with me to wipe them out, all of you. If we don't put out a fire while it is small, it will burn up a haystack as large as Mount Sumeru. Get ready! I will be in command of all the troops."

The next day, the troops of Mandra Sgang assembled. Ha-cang-bdud-mo, in her helmet and armor, was carrying an iron bow and iron arrows and riding a big black horse. She gnashed her long sharp teeth three times. The vicious ministers were excited and the gentle ministers were very sorrowful but could find no way to oppose this. Led by the evil woman, they marched into the kingdom of Padmacan.

People all over Padmacan knew the troops of Mandra Sgang had come, so they assembled outside the palace. The new king said: "The troops coming are with Ha-cang-bdud-mo, my deadly enemy. Today I will command our troops myself to fight the enemy. If I cannot cut out her heart today, she will persecute people all over the world to death."

Everybody believed in this young, brave king of excellent martial skills. Riding on a fast steed, he led his mighty army to fight the enemy. As soon as Ha-cang-bdud-mo saw him coming, she fitted an arrow to her bowstring and took out her knife from its sheath, saying: "When one wants to die, he comes to the gate of the king of hell. If an insect wants to die, he comes to the entrance of an ants' den. Today you want to die, so you bring yourself to my mouth. If I cannot eat you up, my name is not Bdud-mo." With these words, her teeth protruded the length of a hand. She dashed right towards the prince. With his bowstring fully drawn, he shot his arrow straight at her heart and immediately brought her down from her horse. Then the prince galloped to her side, placed his foot upon her and asked: "Look here! Do you recognize me? Do you see that I am Kun-tu-legs-pa?" The evil woman, moving her lips, said: "Your Majesty! You are the deity, the Buddha. Forgive me for my blindness. Pray let me go this time. Let us be real mother and child. You'll be my son. Return to rule over Mandra Sgang and let the princess be the ruler of Padmacan. At least, pray spare my life!"

The prince said: "You forced my mother to go away and made my father insane. You gave my elder sister and me first to the butchers, then to the fishermen and then to the hunters to be put to death. Which of these can I forget? How can I lightly let you go? With these words, knives, spears and clubs came from all directions and beat Ha-cang-bdud-mo into mincemeat. They dug a nine-layer pit on the spot and buried her deep in it. Then they built a pagoda above the pit. The prince sang:

Before the spread of Buddhist teachings,
the demon's witchery could thrive;
Now Buddhist teachings spread far and wide,
All mankind lives in everlasting peace and security.

Later, the prince led some soldiers back to Mandra Sgang, opened the door of the dungeon to set King Ka-la-dbang-po free and exiled Ze-ma-ra-mgo to the wilderness on the frontier. He also found the fishermen, the butchers and the elder hunter, all of whom had been kind to him, and appointed them ministers. Ka-la-dbang-po stayed to be the King of Mandra Sgang and the prince went back to rule over the kingdom of Padmacan.

Ever afterwards, the evil people resolutely corrected their wrongdoings and the good people were learning to become better and better. All was quiet and peaceful throughout the world. Buddhism flourished and spread widely.

MAIDEN GZUGS-KYI-NYI-MA

This script was translated from a lithographic edition, which had many printing errors. A number of corrections were made in the course of translation. The late Tibetan scholar Tsha-sprul-rin-po-che said the opera had been written by a lama from Lho-kha-mon. It appears to have been influenced by the legendary Indian drama "Sakuntala."

In the old days, there was a country whose name, Sems-kyi-blo-gros, means "wisdom of thought." In this country there was a vast, deserted forest, overgrown with brambles, where wild animals roamed. In the forest was an extremely secluded lodge where a hermit lived and meditated in Buddhist austerity.

One day, the hermit saw that the white shawl he had been wearing had become dirty, and he washed it from bank of the river. But, unexpectedly, the dirt that was washed off the shawl flowed along in the water and was drunk by a female deer. The deer became pregnant, and from then on it did not go anywhere else to graze but wandered around the hermit's lodge every day.

The hermit was kind-hearted towards the deer. The months passed. One day, a hundred flowers blossomed, a hundred kinds of grass were luxuriant, a beautiful rainbow appeared in the sky and flowers fell like rain. The sound of melodious music came faintly from some distant place. At this time, the deer gave birth to a beautiful, gentle maiden. The hermit was very fond of her and brought her up at his side. He named her "Gzugs-kyi-nyi-ma."

Now, the king of Sems-kyi-blo-gros was Zla-ba-bde-dpon and the queen was Lha-yi-dpal-mo. They had two sons, the elder one was Zla-ba-seng-ge and the younger one, Zla-ba-blo-gros. As it happened, the two sons had heretical beliefs.

The country was very wealthy and had 36,000 large villages and towns and 95,000 storehouses of treasure. The palace roof was covered with gold tiles, which shone with radiance and dazzled the eye. There were heavenly horses that could fly up to the sky, rhinoceros that could dive into the sea, tame elephants and precious magic oxen and a parrot that could speak fluently and knew everything in the past and future. Indeed, the country enjoyed great wealth and prosperity and had everything that was desirable.

One day, King Zla-ba-bde-dpon brought together his ministers for a consultation. "Lions on the snow mountain might be hit by hurricanes and heavy snow, and tigers in the forest might be hurt by sharp knives and arrows. I, the king, am old and might die. Now I shall abdicate and turn over the throne to a prince. Who, in your opinion, is best suited to be king?"

After a short consultation, the ministers replied as one voice: "The eider prince, Zla-ba-seng-ge, is clever, benevolent and enjoys great popularity among the people. We are willing to have him as our king," and thus the decision was made.

On the day when Zla-ba-seng-ge ascended the throne, people all over the country came to congratulate him, conches and trumpets were blown to mark the occasion, and there was a scene of rejoicing and excitement. After ascending the throne, Zla-ba-seng-ge worshipped Maha-deva, the Great Heaven (the system of heretic beliefs worshipped in accordance with the former king's instructions).

One day when he was returning to his palace from a short journey, King Zla-ba-seng-ge met a bewitching coquettish maiden. At first sight, King Zla-ba-seng-ge was dazzled by her beauty. Unable to refrain from showing his feelings, he stepped forward and asked her: "Maiden, are you the daughter of a god, a dragon, or a human being? If you are not married yet, would you be willing to be my life companion?"

The bewitching maiden answered: "Honorable king, noble king, I am an orphan. I would be very happy even to become your slave."

But one of the ministers in the king's company named A-po-nag-ge knew that this was not a demure maiden, as she seemed, and was afraid that she would make the king muddleheaded and bring disaster to the people. So he came forward to advise the king: "My honorable king, copper cannot be compared with gold, nor a mouse with an elephant. How can a maiden of unknown origin be married to the king?" The king did not listen or pay any attention to these words, but placed the bewitching maiden behind him on his horse and returned to the palace. After that, inauspicious, ominous things often happened in the palace, putting everybody in a constant state of anxiety, wondering what was the cause. The parrot with magical powers advised the king on several occasions to keep apart from the bewitching maiden, who he said was the transformation of a demon. But, infatuated with her beauty, the king ignored the parrot's loyal advice. There was nothing anybody could do about the situation.

The king had a large garden and entrusted a hunter to guard it. One day when the hunter went into the garden, he saw a herd of boars trample the flowers and trees there. The hunter became very angry and, carrying a bow and arrows, chased them. At the sight of the hunter, the boars were panic-stricken and fled for their lives in different directions. The hunter chased closely after a large boar, but on the way he met a river deer. Giving up the boar, the hunter turned around to chase the river deer. After chasing for a long while, he met a David's deer. To the hunter, it was always the other mountain that looked higher. He gave up the river deer at once and chased closely after the David's deer. When he was on the point of catching up with it, he stretched his bow to the full and, with the whizz of an arrow, shot the David's deer.

The David's deer did not fall down but ran away faster instead. The hunter was unwilling to let it go and chased without noticing how far away he was from the palace. The David's deer ran deep into the forest, and the hunter entered in its wake. It was dusk. Finding himself lost and without catching any game, the hunter had to tie himself in a tree and went to sleep.

The next day, he got down from the tree and groped in the forest for a way to go back home. Dashing here and there, he could not find his way out of the forest, and there was nobody there to ask. Suddenly he came to a mirror-like pond and saw that a water bucket had been used on the bank. The hunter pondered: "It seems somebody must live nearby. I will wait for someone to come here, and inquire about the way to return home."

After a while, a maiden came from far away, and was as beautiful as a goddess, light as a swallow, gentle as a flower and kind-hearted as the god of compassion. With a silver ladle in her right hand and a gold water bucket in her left hand, she walked towards the pond. When she came near, the hunter stepped forward and asked, "Divine maiden, you look like a goddess. I am King Zla-ba-seng-ge's gardener. Yesterday I lost my way in my chase after wild animals. Pray be merciful and show me the direction to go home." The maiden gave him a handful of lucky grass and told him to scatter it on the path and he would get home without question.

The hunter scattered the lucky grass on the path and indeed returned to the palace. He immediately went to see the king.

But the king was playing merrily with his many imperial concubines, and the hunter found it difficult to tell his story in plain language. So he asked a riddle:

"Honorable king, you can tie down the Seven-Sister Star in heaven if you have the goddess-binding rope; you can get the treasures of the dragon palace in the sea if you know how. Noble king, just look at my face and you'll understand."

When the king heard the hunter's riddle, he guessed that the hunter must have found a good maiden for him. So he went in disguise to the hunter and asked more about his story. What he learned made him very happy, and he went with the hunter all the way along the path he scattered with lucky grass, in search of the maiden.

The hunter and the king ran all the way until they were breathless. Finally, they arrived at the edge of the pond where the hunter had been the previous day. After a while, the maiden appeared. When the king gazed at her carefully, he found her indeed beautiful beyond compare. The queen and imperial concubines in his palace all seemed as dust to him. So he stepped forward and spoke to her: "Lovely, goddess-like, beautiful maiden, I am King Zla-ba-seng-ge. At the first sight of you I could not tear myself away from you?' He had not finished his words before the maiden ran off, disappearing in an instant just like a young deer that had met a hunter. The king and the hunter were helpless and had to sleep in a tree beside the pond for another night.

The following day when the maiden came to fetch water, the king stepped forward again to speak to her: "Lha-mo (angel) in the forest, if you promise to become my queen, you will live in a palace of comfort,

91

wear silks and satins, eat many kinds of fruits, drink liquid sweet as dew, and watch dances in costumes in a riot of colors and listen to celestial music. My country has 36,000 large villages and towns, heavenly steeds that can soar across the skies, rhinoceros that can dive into the sea. No wealth, rank and prosperity in the world are higher and greater than mine. Maiden, won't you go along with me?"

The maiden listened and dipped up water in silence. When the bucket was full, she again ran off and vanished in an instant, just like the day before. Later, following her footsteps, the king and the hunter chased after her up to a hermit's thatched shed.

This hermit had profound religious attainments and was leading a life of meditation and austerity. The king quickly knelt, bowed and paid him homage. He told the hermit in detail the purpose of his arrival and asked for his help. The hermit said, "The maiden you met is probably my adopted daughter Gzugs-kyi-nyi-ma. She is the incarnation of the goddess who came down to earth after having borrowed the womb of a female deer as the site of pregnancy. It will not be difficult for you to marry her and make her your queen. If you can give up the heretic beliefs you formerly worshipped and be converted to Buddhist teaching, your wish will be fulfilled."

Hearing this, the king was overjoyed, kowtowed many times and promised to give 500 ounces of gold to support the hermit. He pledged to reject all heretic beliefs and be converted to Buddhism from then on.

The hermit called Gzugs-kyi-nyi-ma to his side and instructed her: "My child! Now you are going away to become the queen and spread the Buddhist teachings. No greater beneficence can be achieved. This is a marriage destined by your previous incarnation. Later, some vicious people will plot against you. I am giving you a necklace that will ward off evil spirits and subdue demons. You must wear it carefully on your body and never tell anyone about it, not even your husband. In this way you'll enjoy happiness and security all your life."

King Zla-ba-seng-ge returned with Gzugs-kyi-nyi-ma to the palace and immediately conferred on her the title of queen. They were a very affectionate couple, enjoying deep conjugal love. The king forgot all about his former queen and imperial concubines.

Gzugs-kyi-nyi-ma was honest, tolerant and kind-hearted. She was simple and always spoke gently, winning the admiration and esteem of ministers and people all over the country.

The king's former 2,500 imperial concubines were very jealous of Gzugs-kyi-nyi-ma, but especially envious was the bewitching woman brought back by the king some time ago. They often gathered to plot against Gzugs-kyi-nyi-ma. The bewitching woman played the chief role in the plot. They found on the street a witch named Yamangende, a woman with a good command of magic and vicious tricks. Ordinarily she went to this family and that in the streets. She was skillful at playing wind and stringed instruments, singing and dancing and excelled in cunning, mischievous schemes. It is difficult to say how many crimes she had committed.

After the 2,500 imperial concubines had found Yamangende, they prized her as a treasure. In particular, the bewitching woman entertained her with most generous hospitality. Finally, she proposed that the witch try to kill Gzugs-kyi-nyi-ma. Without hesitation, the witch, beating her chest, guaranteed that Gzugs-kyi-nyi-ma would die at her hand.

Yamangende, carrying a twelve-stringed instrument, sang and performed at the gate of the palace. King Zla-ba-seng-ge heard her and sent attendants to fetch her into the palace for a performance. The witch demonstrated all her skills, playing so melodiously as to pierce the clouds and split rocks and dancing as gracefully as if many golden snakes were swirling. The king was much pleased and sent her to wait upon Gzugs-kyi-nyi-ma.

As soon as she saw Gzugs-kyi-nyi-ma, Yamangende, with a tongue like a snake, flattered her with an extravagantly colorful description of the sky raining flowers. The witch instantly won her heart and Gzugs-kyi-nyi-ma took her as a bosom friend.

That very night, the witch secretly placed paper with magic incantations and different kinds of poison in the palace where Gzugs-kyi-nyi-ma lived. She thought that the queen would die, become insane or fall ill. But, to her astonishment, on the following day when the witch went to Gzugs-kyi-nyi-ma's palace, she found her as healthy and as serene as ever. Because Yamangende had boasted of her power, she was both angry and impatient. She could think of nothing else to do, so she chatted quietly with Gzugs-kyi-nyi-ma and said in a soft voice, "I think you should take good care of yourself. Somebody may be jealous of you and secretly plot against you!"

Gzugs-kyi-nyi-ma was very grateful to her and replied with great assurance, "Dear friend, thank you for your attentions. I am not afraid of anybody's secret plotting because I have a pearl necklace to protect me." When Yamangende went back to the bewitching woman she told her to take out some pearls quickly and thread them into a necklace. The following day she took it to Gzugs-kyi-nyi-ma and said hypocritically: "You are really lucky to have a magic pearl necklace. It's because you did charitable and pious deeds and formed ties of kindness in your previous incarnation. Would you please take off the necklace and let me do homage to it? It would be a charitable deed on your part to let it bestow some blessing on me! "

Gzugs-kyi-nyi-ma forgot the hermit's instructions. Besides, she should not have indiscreetly trusted the witch and taken the pearl necklace from her neck. Yamangende pretended to be astonished at its beauty, stroked it over and over again and stealthily replaced it with the fake pearl necklace she had brought. Then she took out a magic drug and spread it, making Gzugs-kyi-nyi-ma unconscious as if she were drunk.

The scheming witch carried a human corpse from the graveyard that very night, cut it into halves and put the internal organs by Gzugs-kyi-nyi-ma's pillow, and smeared human blood on her face and hands while she was sleeping. Only then did the witch sneak away. Gzags-kyi-nyi-ma knew nothing about all this.

The following day when the sun shone over the snow mountain, King Zla-ba-seng-ge did not see Gzugs-kyi-nyi-ma and thought that she had fallen ill. He hastened to visit her at the palace where she lived. As soon as he entered the room, he was stunned by the sight of blood and flesh. Then he saw Gzugs-kyi-nyi-ma's face stained with blood and there was still a trace of blood on her mouth. With anger rising in his breast, he said: "I thought you were a goddess. Suddenly, I find you a demon. I will send you to the nether world!" With that, he lifted his sword and was going to slash her. Suddenly, the parrot with magical powers flew to his side, shouting aloud: "Don't be rash! Don't be rash!" The king asked, "Would it be rash if I killed this demon?"

The parrot said: "Let me tell you a story: In the old days, a hunter went hunting in the hills. On his way, he was both hungry and thirsty. Suddenly a spring flowed down in front of him. The hunter was very pleased and hurriedly ran forward to drink the water. At that moment a crow flew to his side, flapping its wings against his eyes, and repeatedly prevented him from drinking the water. The hunter was extremely angry, strung an arrow to his bow and shot the crow dead. Later on, he turned over the matter in his mind: Why did the crow try to prevent me from drinking the water? There must be something queer in this! So he went to inspect the upper current of the spring and saw that a snake was dripping poisonous saliva, drop by drop, into the water. Only then did the hunter realize that he should not have killed the crow. Say, do you have to think carefully about a matter before taking action?"

The king said, "According to what you have said, I should be more careful!" So he wakened Gzugs-kyi-nyi-ma, who, as if waking from a dream, knew nothing about what had happened.

A few days later, Yamangende again came to Gzugs-kyi-nyi-ma's presence and made her fall into unconsciousness with a magic drug, the same as before. Then she cut off the nose of the king's favorite elephant, put it beside Gzugs-kyi-nyi-ma's pillow and smeared her face, hands and mouth with fresh blood, and sneaked away. The following day, King Zla-ba-seng-ge heard that the elephant's nose had been cut off and saw Gzugs-kyi-nyi-ma's bloodstained face. Filled with anger, he again pulled out his sword and was going to kill her. Just then the magic parrot flew to his side again, saying: "Don't be rash!" Then it told the following story: "In old days, a woman went uphill hunting and left her child at home for the family cat to look after. When she was gone, a huge python came and tried to eat the child. The cat wrestled desperately with the python and bit and killed it. When the woman returned, the cat went outdoors to greet her. As soon as she saw its mouth and claws covered with blood, she thought that the cat had eaten her child. In a surge of anger she killed the cat with an ax. When she went into her house she saw the dead python and her child safe and sound. Only then it dawned on her that she had done something wrong."

After the king heard this story, he put down his sword and wakened Gzugs-kyi-nyi-ma. Again she felt as if she had come from a dream and knew nothing about what had happened.

A few days later, Yamangende came again to the queen and made her unconscious with a magic drug. Then she stealthily went and killed the king's younger brother, Zla-ba-blo-gros, put his heart by Gzugs-kyi-nyi-ma's pillow and smeared her face, mouth and hands with blood. Then she sneaked away.

When King Zla-ba-seng-ge saw his beloved brother killed and eaten by Gzugs-kyi-nyi-ma, he could no longer restrain himself, but just as he was drawing the sword to kill her, the parrot with magic powers again flew to his side to plead for her. But this time, the king scolded without allowing it time to speak: "You, damned devil, have always fooled me with sweet words. Listening to you, I have lost my beloved younger brother. If I listen to your words again, I am afraid both my country and my life will be in danger." With these words, he pierced the parrot with his sword and killed it.

But as he looked at Gzugs-kyi-nyi-ma's flower-like countenance and recalled the days of their wedded love, the king could not bring himself to kill her with his own hands, no matter how hard he tried. Consequently, he ordered three butchers to take her to the Sea of Seething Blood to be tormented.

The three cruel butchers escorted Gzugs-kyi-nyi-ma to the Sea of Seething Blood. Along the way, people of all the villages and towns were sympathetic to her misfortunes and stood on the roadside to greet and comfort her. Some even expressed their determination to go to the capital to plead on her behalf. If necessary, they said, they would kill several villains to redress the injustice and avenge her. Some elderly people felt sorry for her, beating their chests and stamping their feet. But Gzugs-kyi-nyi-ma consoled them one by one, telling them not to feel sorry for her and that rights and wrongs, truth and falsehood, were bound to be clarified in the long run. Walking behind the three butchers, she went on towards the Sea of Seething Blood.

On the way, the two younger of the three butchers began to think they should not do such an unkind and unjust act, that it would indeed be a sin to let righteous Gzugs-kyi-nyi-ma be tormented. So they sneaked away and left it to the old butcher to do the inhuman deed alone. Obsessed with the desire for gain, the old butcher wanted to win a prize from the king, so he escorted Gzugs-kyi-nyi-ma right to the edge and, tying her up with ropes, he threw her into the filthy, stinking Sea of Seething Blood.

Gzugs-kyi-nyi-ma underwent all sorts of torment in the Sea of Seething Blood, but in her heart she prayed: "My esteemed Triratna (the triad of the Buddha, the dharma, and the sangha), I am in torment and suffering here, hit by misfortune for an unknown reason in the disastrous months of the year. I wish to experience all human suffering. I wish all other people could be free of disaster. I wish all living creatures would always love one another and enjoy peace and happiness."

Her devotion moved all the local guardian deities and they all came to protect her, and helped her get out of the Sea of Seething Blood and once again walk along the road that led to the capital. She disguised herself as a nun and on her way expounded Buddhist scriptures and teachings and spread Buddhist philosophy. What a great number of people were inspired by her and converted to Buddhism. Her reputation spread farther and farther. Even people in the capital heard of this nun of profound purity and her good command of Buddhist scriptures and teachings.

Meanwhile, since King Zla-ba-seng-ge had driven Gzugs-kyi-nyi-ma away, unlucky omens often appeared in the palace and drought and famine followed. Avalanches, landslides, floods and locusts plunged the country into an abyss of misery and chaos. When the king heard that a nun of profound spirituality had arrived, he went in disguise with the hunter and minister A-po-nag-ge to listen to her expounding Buddhist teachings. At the same time, the scheming imperial consort and the witch Yamangende also came to give alms to the nun so as to purge the deadly sins they had committed. But none of them knew that the nun was Gzugs-kyi-nyi-ma, against whom they had plotted in former times. The king and the others saw the consort and Yaman-gende kneeling at the feet of the nun to make confessions. They hid themselves nearby to listen; thus, they heard the two women tell, with tears of repentance, how they had planned and carried out their scheme, how the witch cheated Gzugs-kyi-nyi-ma to get the magic pearl necklace and how she killed the young prince. When Gzugs-kyi-nyi-ma heard this frank confession, tears streamed down her face and she was choked with sobbing. At that moment, King Zla-ba-seng-ge, who listened nearby, bristled with anger, and his rage spread like a forest fire. He stepped forward, grasped the consort and the witch and drew his sword to kill them. Luckily, Gzugs-kyi-nyi-ma bravely came forward and prevented the king from doing so, saying, "Your Majesty, you are brave as a lion and as perfect as the full moon. Let bygones be bygones, like the drifting sands. We should look to the future, and all things will grow as bountifully as green grass. Fortunately, thanks to the Buddha's protection, I escaped from their vicious plot unscathed. Today I am here, safe and sound. Please forgive them and let them mend their ways!"

When the king saw that the nun was Gzugs-kyi-nyi-ma, he was astonished and overjoyed, though he was also ashamed. At his repeated entreaties, she agreed to return to the palace and once again became queen. Later she gave birth to a crown prince named Nyi-ma-seng-ge. From then on, withered trees blossomed, men and animals thrived and people all over the land led a happy life.

BROTHERS DON-YOD
AND DON-GRUB

The basic content of this opera is contained in the book "An Endless Story." (The original title was "A Story Told by a Fantastic Corpse." Its Tibetan editions consist of the Sde-dge woodblock edition and the hand-copied editions from several places. They vary from 21 chapters to 15 or 13, and do not have quite the same content but all contain this story. It seems to have spread fairly widely.

As the script of a Tibetan opera, the story appears in two editions printed by woodblock, one entitled "The Secret History of Pan-chen-blo-bzang-yes-shes" and the other with the title "Story of Brothers Don-yod and Don-grub."

Once upon a time, there was a country named Stod-pa-bsam-gling. Its king, who was called Pa-la-de-va, married Princess Kun-bzang-ma, daughter of King Shi-ba-dra of another country. They were very affectionate and led a harmonious, happy life. But after quite a number of years, she had borne neither a son nor a daughter. The king worried very much about descendants, and went often to pray to gods and consult the oracle, the prophets and the fortune-tellers here and there.

One day, a famous sorcerer of the country was invited to consult the oracle. The sorcerer told the king: "Beyond an island in the open sea there is an islet named Go-sha-gling where a mystic dragon lives.

If you devoutly offer sacrifices to him, you may possibly get some children."

The king thanked him for the advice and departed with his queen, his ministers and commoners for the journey, all dressed in gorgeous costumes. They traveled straight to their destination, with offerings for the gods loaded on elephants. After arriving at the seaside, they sailed on ships for five days and nights and came to the place of the mystic dragon, on the islet. They stayed there for seven days, paying homage to the dragon each day, in accordance with the custom.

On the seventh night, King Pa-la-de-va dreamed that A-tsi-ra (reciter of Tantric incantations) came into his presence holding a rosary in his hands and said to him: "Pa-la-de-va, you seem to be a devout person. Soon you may get two princes as successors to your throne: One is the incarnation of Avalokitesvara (the God of Mercy) and the other is the incarnation of the god of wisdom. Now you should rejoice!"

Of course these words made the king very happy, and he asked the reciter, "Who are you?"

"I am the god who is the ruler of Paradise in the Western Heavens, Vod-dpag-med (Infinite Light). The guardian god of you and your son is the Immortal of Go-sha-gling, Va-nj-mu-nj. You must come often to offer him sacrifices."

When the king woke up, he saw other auspicious signs and was even more delighted. Tidying up his things, he returned to the palace.

After nine months and ten days, Queen Kun-bzang-ma did indeed give birth to a prince. At the time of his birth, flowers from heaven rained down and a rainbow appeared like a canopy over the earth. A grand banquet was held in the palace for a celebration, along with blowing conches, raising flags, ringing bells and beating drums. The sorcerer was given an ample reward. As the king had all his wishes satisfied, he named this prince Don-grub, which means "success and perfection."

When the prince reached the age of five, he could recite from memory the six-word philosophical saying Om-ma-ni-pad-mal-hum, "Hail to the jewel in the lotus!" (Equivalent to the Lord's Prayer, especially in Latin.) Everybody was surprised at this.

Unexpectedly, that year, Queen Kun-bzang-ma suddenly contracted a serious illness. Praying, consulting oracles, taking medicine and acupuncture all proved ineffective. She died, leaving behind her husband and son. People all over the country, high and low, grieved.

A year later, the king and his son went to attend a ceremony celebrating the completion of a pagoda. The king spotted a maiden in the crowd—she was charming and bewitching. After sending his emissaries to inquire about her, he learned that she was Pad-mo-can, the daughter of an ordinary family. He ordered his ministers to bring her to the palace, where he married her and made her queen, and lavished his love on her.

One night, the king again dreamed that the Infinite Light was bringing him a prince. Indeed, the queen became pregnant. After nine months and ten days, she bore a prince. Because the child came from a noteworthy family, the king named him Don-yod, which means "attaining enlightenment."

While Prince Don-yod was growing up, he was unwilling to live with his mother or his wet nurse, but wanted to spend every day with his elder brother, Don-grub, studying, playing, taking meals and resting together. The king was very pleased with such fraternal affection as theirs.

Several years passed. One day, the queen opened a window of the palace and gazed into the east. She saw many people singing operas and dancing on the eastern square. She heard them say: "Our king has two princes. Prince Don-grub is of fine quality and good temper and was borne by a princess. He should be designated the successor to the throne in the future. As for Don-yod, he is also acceptable but his mother is a person of unknown origin. He must not be allowed to inherit the throne!"

Listening to these words, the queen was much displeased. She banged the eastern window shut and opened another window to gaze to the south. She saw many men engaged in horse racing and archery on the southern square, and it was a bustling scene too. But she heard people saying: "Elder Prince Don-grub is really the person eligible to inherit the throne. Although the younger Prince Don-yod is not bad, he is inferior to his elder brother." Listening to these words, the queen became more impatient. She banged shut the southern window and opened another window to gaze to the north. She saw many children playing hide-and-seek. In a short time, the children heaped up a pile of stones to be a throne. One boy, decking himself out as Prince Don-grub, sat on the throne. Many other boys, dressing themselves up as ministers, kowtowed to him. Other children in the guise of ordinary people took off their clothes and, tying up their sleeves, dragged them forward on the ground as if they were offerings of oxen and sheep. Another boy, decked out as Prince Don-yod, sat on a straw cushion at one side. Looking at this, the queen was shocked. She said to herself: "Don't discount Don-grub. Although his mother is dead, he still has considerable influence! Judging by what I have seen today, very likely he will take over the throne someday and there is no hope for my son Don-yod. If my son cannot become king, then I, his mother, will be an insignificant person! I must use my head."

A few days later, she smeared some red clay on her right cheek and some indigo color on her left cheek, disguising herself as a mad woman and made a clamor. The king became very worried and asked what was the matter with her. She deliberately did not answer. The king was alarmed and frightened, and invited fortune tellers to interpret the oracle, and lamas to recite Buddhist sutras and sorcerers to pray to avert disaster. But all proved ineffective. The king was so worried that he himself almost felt sick. Thus, three days passed. The king came to the queen's bedside, asking: "Dear Pad-mo-can, do you yourself know some way to cure your ailment?"

She said, "There is a method, but you cannot carry it out. You had better let me die! No need to say any more!" Again she pretended to groan. The king said: "No matter how many wild beasts there are in the mountains, they will always fall prey to lions. No matter how many affairs there are in the world, they can always be managed by a king. Speak quickly. Let me carry it out!"

"Unless you take an oath, I won't believe that you can really carry it out," said the queen, and the king unhesitatingly took an oath, saying: "Dkon-mchog-gsum (a Tibetan oath, invoking the triad of the Buddha, the dharma, and the sangha)."

Then the queen said, "Our elder prince Don-grub is the reincarnation of a demon. Shortly after he was born, he harassed his own mother Kun-bzang-ma to death. Now he is tormenting me. It seems I cannot live long, but it doesn't matter whether or not I die. I am afraid it's your turn to die next. If it is possible to seize and kill this transformation of a demon, my ailment will, without doubt, be cured and there will be no need to worry about your life."

Hearing this, the king was very shocked, and thought to himself: "I got this Prince Don-grub of mine by praying to gods and the Buddha. People say he has an unusual countenance and is suitable to inherit the throne. I don't think he is a demon, but it was also true that Kun-bzang-ma died without any cause. What a great misfortune it would be if I allowed my beloved queen to die again! I cannot bear to kill my son Don-grub with my own hands. Let it be, let it be, let it be! Let me exile him to a desolate frontier. Then the queen's ailment will be cured." He told the queen this idea, and she was fully satisfied.

So the king issued an order that Prince Don-grub be sent to a desolate frontier, and the two brothers soon heard of it. Don-yod said to Don-grub: "Elder brother! If you are going to a desolate frontier, pray take me with you. I want to go with you. I will go wherever you go!"

Don-grub said: "My good brother! Pray listen to me. I am going to the wilderness neither for a trip nor for a pilgrimage. There are many dangers on the way, as well as hunger and wandering. Don't go with me. Stay at home and obey the instructions of your father and mother and you will inherit the throne and rule our country someday."

But Don-yod sobbed, "Elder brother, how can I stay here alone to inherit the throne when you are going to suffer in the wilderness? Pray take me along! Live or die, I want to be with you!" However hard Dong-grub tried to advise Don-yod, he would not listen. Finally, Don-grub gave up.

One night, Don-grub stealthily got out of bed and was going to depart. But Don-yod suspected what he was going to do and hugged his neck tightly, refusing to loosen his grip, sobbing and crying.

Don-grub had to wait until his brother had fallen asleep. Then, carrying his dry grain and beef on his back, he sneaked out of the palace and marched straight towards the northern frontier wilderness.

When Don-yod woke up and found his elder brother gone, he traced his footprints, sobbing and shouting: "Elder brother! Elder brother!" When Don-grub heard his younger brother's shouting he sighed and waited for Don-yod to catch up with him. Then the two brothers set off together for the frontier wilderness.

When several of the more kindly ministers found out about this, they were very concerned and secretly sent three servants with elephants and horses to go with the brothers and look after them on the way. Thus, they all marched for more than half a month until they arrived at the frontier of their country. The servants could not continue anymore, so Don-grub sent them back. They were very reluctant to part with the brothers and were much grieved and wept. Although Don-grub was sad, he advised them:

Everybody must be responsible for himself,
There is no need for others to take his part,
Separation lies at the end of gathering,
Whether for traveling merchants,
Or dark clouds hiding the moon,
Or money that passes through our hands without
    benefiting us,
Pray go back, the three of you,
We may meet again in the future.

But the three servants were still unwilling to begin their return journey, feeling reluctant to part with the brothers.

Don-grub again said:
The beauty of youth is as transient as a colorful rainbow,
Life resembles flowers that do not last long;
Let us pledge to one another we'll meet in heaven in the future.

With these words, the brothers proceeded straight to the frontier wilderness.

Meanwhile, when the king and queen found out that the brothers had both gone away, they were very worried. They sent officials to look for them everywhere, but it was like fallen leaves drifting in the woods, pebbles sunk into the sea and the mist dispersed in the sky. Not even their shadows could be found. The queen, who had pretended to be sick, was now, indeed, severely ill because her beloved son had disappeared. All the people were worried about the princes.

Don-grub and Don-yod went past sparse villages, herdsmen's black yurts, a vast expanse of desert and large dense forests, until they came to a completely desolate place where nobody lived. They had eaten up the dry grain they had brought and even the leather sack for storing it. Their mouths felt as dry as fire. Their limbs were weak and numb, and they had to sit down and rest.

Don-grub spotted some fruit on a tree, picked them and gave them to Don-yod. Only then did they again walk on, dragging their feet. When they came to Ox Nose Hill, Don-yod was not able to continue the journey. Don-grub bade him sit down for a rest. He himself tried to search for water on the other side of the hill. After walking a great distance, he found a ditch that had dried up, and an empty pond. Looking back, he saw that his younger brother had fallen to the ground. Dong-grub gave up his search for water, ran back to his brother and found him almost dying, like a withered flower. When Don-grub hugged him and lifted him up, Don-yod opened his eyes and said, "Elder brother! I am afraid I can no longer go with you. You must take good care of your health!" Don-grub's heart was as distressed as if stabbed by a knife. He carried his dying brother in his arms, with his tears streaming down like a fountain.

At this moment, a cuckoo and a nightingale flew up to the brothers and circled around, as though praying for them. After a time, Don-yod closed his eyes and stopped breathing. Mountains and peaks in all directions shook and flowers rained down from the sky; melodious music sounded faintly in the air. Many wild beasts—tigers, monkeys and apes—came down from the mountains and did not threaten Don-grub but seemed to protect him instead.

Don-grub wept for a while and then, carrying his brother's corpse on his back, went on. After he had crossed eight mountains, he came to a large forest where sandalwood trees spread all over the mountain and milk flowed in a river. Don-grub thought: "There is no other place as good as this. Let me bury my brother here!" He placed Don-yod's body well under a large umbrella-shaped sandalwood tree and encircled it with many pieces of sandalwood so that it would always stay in this spot. Then he himself walked on towards the northern frontier wilderness, step by step.

As he again crossed thirteen mountains, Don-grub saw a Buddhist streamer fluttering at the tip of a tree. He thought: "Wherever a Buddhist streamer flutters there must be a village or perhaps a herdsmen's yurt, or at least some people and some grain." So he walked towards the Buddhist streamer. Near a forest halfway up the mountain, he saw people's footprints on the ground and his mind soothed. After some time he emerged from the woods onto a vast grassland. He thought he heard someone reciting a Buddhist sutra there. He thought there must certainly be a temple nearby.

Don-grub climbed on up the mountain and came to a clear, sparkling pond. Beside it was a white-haired old lama reciting sutras and incantations while throwing an offering made of butter and roasted barley meal into the pond. Prince Don-grub bowed and made his obeisance, saying: "Living Buddha, pray give me guidance...." Without waiting for him to finish, the old lama turned to look at him and was very surprised. He asked, "Are you a man or a ghost?" For Prince Don-grub was as thin as a skeleton and was disheveled. He looked more like a ghost than a human being, after his long, strenuous journey. He had braved wind and damp, without enough food or sleep, and he was weighed down with grief over Don-yod's death. He said:

"Living Buddha. Pray look at me with your eyes of wisdom. I am not a ghost but a man who has met a disaster!"

The lama again asked: "If you are not a ghost, then where have you come from and where are you going?"

Don-grub answered, "I have come from far away to undergo hardships here!" As the young man was truly pitiable, the lama led him to a mountain cave. First, he bade him take a bath, cut short his hair and change into a suit of clean clothes. Then the lama cooked some food for him. While Don-grub was eating, the lama inquired where he had come from and about his family origin. As he talked about what had saddened him, Don-grub's tears streamed down. Even the lama felt sorry for him.

Later, Don-grub honored the lama as his master and served him in the mountain cave. Every day he rose early, fetching water and gathering firewood. He picked special soft grass to make a cushion for the lama. But the lama saw that he still had a sorrowful face, so he asked the prince: "Don-grub, is something still weighing on your mind?"

"Living Buddha," answered the prince. "I have settled down here but my miserable younger brother is far away from me and I cannot find even his body. I can never set my mind at ease until I find his corpse and bring it here."

The lama said: "This is what you ought to do! You need not worry. I'll escort you in this search." The master and disciple departed in search of Prince Don-yod's corpse.

Meanwhile, Prince Don-yod, dying of thirst, had been placed by Prince Don-grub under a sandalwood tree. Unexpectedly, a heavy rain fell in the night and rainwater dripped down from the sandalwood tree onto his face and flowed to the corner of his mouth. Slowly it moistened his throat. Like the crops receiving a pleasant rain in a year of drought, Prince Don-yod slowly regained consciousness. Some say he was revived by two gods, Lha-tshangs-pa and Lha-khyab-vjug. Ah ya! He felt as though he had just wakened from a dream. He looked around and saw that he was surrounded by trees. Where had Dong-grub gone?

Don-yod shouted aloud: "Elder brother, Elder brother!" But, except for an echo from the mountain valley, nobody answered him. Don-yod thought: "Alas! Some disaster has happened. Can it be that some wild beast has harmed my elder brother? How sorry I am that I haven't helped him!" Jumping up hurriedly, he stumbled into the forest shouting, "Brother! Elder brother! Where are you? Where are you?" He kept on shouting, and when he was hungry, he ate some fruit and when he got thirsty, he drank a little water, and continued to search for elder brother Don-grub.

Don-grub and his master arrived at the place where Don-yod's corpse had been placed. There they saw that the original heap of wood was scattered and some fruit peelings lay on the ground, as if somebody had been there. But Don-yod's body had disappeared like a rainbow in the sky. Don-grub was even more grieved and thought perhaps Don-yod's body had been ravaged by wild beasts. He searched everywhere for seven days, but could find no trace of it.

The old lama advised him: "Child, don't make your efforts in vain! I think your younger brother must have been saved and taken away by some god, and you will have a chance to meet again in the future. Don't be so worried and sad or your health will be affected!" Don-grub believed his master's words and returned with the old lama to the mountain cave.

The lama said to him: "Soon I will go to the palace of a king near here, to recite sutras. You should also learn some rites and the recitation of Buddhist sutras." So Don-grub learned Buddhist sutras from the lama and did not leave the mountain for a long time.

One day, when Prince Don-grub came down the mountain to buy some utensils, he saw many shepherd boys playing and rollicking on a plain at the opening of a mountain valley. He joined their play, and all the children liked him and chose him as leader in this or that game. When he returned to the mountain cave, the master asked him why he was so late. He told his master the truth and the master advised him: "Watch out, don't tell others your family background lest you bring some trouble on yourself." Don-grub promised to be careful.

A few days later, he went down the mountain to buy grain and again played with the children. The children held a contest of strength but no one could rival Don-grub. The other children asked why he had such great strength. He said, "It's because I was born in the year of dragon. Can a dragon be weak?" So the children called him "Born in the Year of Dragon," and this nickname became very popular.

This place was under King Go-cha's jurisdiction. The palace was far away from the mountain, a magnificent building hemmed in by hundreds of thousands of households. The king had only one daughter, a princess beautiful as a fairy maiden and gentle as a sheep. The king cherished her like a pearl in his palm.

There was a large lake inside this country, where lived a dragon king. When the fifteenth day of the sixth month arrived each summer, the mystic dragon colored like jadeite danced in the sky with rumbling thunder and flashing lightning. The king led his officials and commoners to the lake to offer sacrifices to the mystic dragon. This guaranteed favorable weather for crops every year and both people and animals enjoyed peace.

Later, for some unknown reason, epidemics and floods occurred in the country and many people and animals died. According to the plan of a sorcerer, the king ordered a boy born in the year of dragon to be thrown into the lake as a sacrifice to the dragon king, in exchange for the country's peace and prosperity. Many boys born in that country in the year of dragon were sacrificed and others fled; none dared to stay home to wait for death.

This year, the time came again for offering sacrifices to the mystic dragon, but however hard the officials tried, they could not find a boy born in the year of dragon. The king was very worried and ordered minister Tri-shod to go around and make a search.

Tri-shod was a cunning, sinister and ruthless fellow; he envied and hated others. Killing was his only hobby. Throwing a boy into the lake every year was always his business. Nobody knew how many boys died at his hands. When he learned from a group of children that Don-grub had been born in the year of dragon, he hastened to report this to the king, who ordered him to go and arrest Don-grub.

When the large contingent of people led by Tri-shod entered the forest, the lama already saw what was going on. He knew that when an owl enters a house, it means more bad than good luck, and when soldiers enter a common house, it means more hardship than goodwill. He hastily told Don-grub to hide in a heap of straw and covered it with a broken earthen jar. He bade him never to come out of the jar unless he was told to do so; otherwise, he would be in danger of death.

Minister Tri-shod entered the cave and, grabbing the old lama, said, "Hey, old man! I hear you have a son born in the year of dragon. Now the king has ordered me to arrest him. Where is he? Speak quickly!"

The old lama said: "My lord, I am a monk. How can I have a son? I am an ascetic Buddhist disciple here, a lonely man without a companion."

Refusing to listen, Tri-shod said again, "You lie! I'll show you how formidable the government is!"

The old lama said calmly, "Even if you kill me, I can tell you nothing. What shall I say?"

Without further argument, Tri-shod pushed the old lama into the cave and, calling his attendants, prepared to torture him. Taking out a knife, he brandished its bright sharp blade this way and that way. It was truly ferocious.

Don-grub, hiding in the straw heap, saw all these things and thought to himself: "I cannot let my master suffer for my sake. Besides, he is very old. How can he stand up to such torture?" So he suddenly jumped out of the straw heap and said, "Hey! Don't make the old man suffer! I am here!"

Tri-shod said with a sneer: "Ah ha. A good little fellow. It's you." He grabbed Don-grub and tied him up tightly and took him back to the palace. As they left, he said to the old lama: "Such a good Buddhist monk. Where has such a big son come from?" With these words, he hit the lama's chest with his fist, making him fall to the ground on his back. Then he swaggered off, whistling. The old lama, with tears in his eyes, could only pray silently to the gods and the Buddha to protect Don-grub.

After Don-grub had been taken by force to the palace, the first person who saw him was the princess. She was especially taken by this handsome youth and asked the king to let him play with her. The king always approved whatever the princess said and never refused anything she asked. So he consented. Seeing that Prince Don-grub was dignified and impressive in appearance, the king was inclined to like him too. So he permitted them to play together.

Seven days later, when it was time to offer sacrifices to the lake and for Tri-shod to take Don-grub away, the princess wept and begged the king to change the decision. The king also thought it was a pity to throw such a handsome young lad into the lake to feed the dragon, and said to Tri-shod: "Go find another boy born in the year of dragon to replace him!"

But Tri-shod shook his head and said:

The king cannot break his promise,

Breaking his promise would make him a laughing-stock;

Words spoken by the king resemble an arrow shot,

It can never be turned back;

Words spoken by the king resemble a bird set free,

It can never be brought back;

Words spoken by the king resemble water flowing away,

It can never be reversed.

You had better allow me to take him away!

Listening to these words, the king could find no way to refute him, and was in a dilemma. The princess at his side wept sorrowfully.

At this moment, Don-grub thought to himself: "If I don't go as a sacrifice to the dragon king, I am afraid another boy born in the year of dragon will die. I cannot cause others suffering for the sake of my own happiness." So he turned and said, "Your Majesty, Princess. Don't trouble yourselves about me. You'd better let me go!" But the princess would by no means allow him to go.

So the king let the two sail together in a boat towards the middle of the dragon lake. When the princess became sleepy and was dozing, Don-grub jumped into the mirror-like lake. She was startled and woke up, but it was too late to save Don-grub and she had to return to the palace, weeping bitterly.

After Don-grub had plunged into the water, he arrived in a trance at the entrance of a splendid palace. A group of shrimp soldiers and crab generals grabbed him and took him to the dragon palace, where the dragon king, dragon queen, dragon children and dragon grandchildren were gathered, waiting for this sumptuous "feast." When they saw that the boy sent this time was so handsome, so brave and without a trace of fear, they asked about his family and his history. Dong-grub told them all about his past, from birth on, including the disasters that had befallen him, his younger brother's death, parting with the lama, and the princess' love for him.

When they heard all these things, the mystic dragons were astonished and respectful. They sighed for him and were very sympathetic, and thought well of his spirit of self-sacrifice, so they invited him into the dragon palace and entertained him with warm hospitality.

Don-grub lived in the dragon palace for three months and explained to them Buddhist teachings, brotherhood and the importance of respecting the aged and helping the young. All the mystic dragon gods were moved. They took oaths they would never eat human beings again and never conjure up storms and tempestuous waves to harm people. They also gave Don-grub many treasures as gifts, including large pearls and countless pieces of jade, agate, coral and jadeite.

The dragon king told the prince to close his eyes and think of wherever he wanted to go. Prince Don-grub thought: "I am going to visit my master. I wonder how it has fared with him."

As soon as this idea cropped up, he heard the sound of water and found himself at the mountain cave. He saw his master sitting upright on a rush cushion, reciting sutras. The prince called gently: "Master!" The old lama raised his head and saw him, and was so astonished and happy that he fainted away. Don-grub hastened to spray sandalwood water on the lama's face and he regained consciousness.

The old lama said, "Can it be that we meet each other in a dream?"

Don-grub told all his experiences to the master and took out all the jewels and treasures he had brought from the dragon palace to provide for the support of his master. After this tribulation, the master and the disciple were even more devoted to each other, eating from the same vessel, and always sitting side by side.

King Go-cha saw that after Don-grub had been thrown into the lake, his country truly enjoyed peace and harvested rich grain crops. But he felt sorry for the old lama, believing he had wronged the venerable one. So he sent minister Chos-dpal-ba-dpal to the mountain to invite the old lama to the palace to be provided for and looked after. The lama could not refuse, but he was reluctant to leave Don-grub alone on the mountain. If he took Don-grub along, he was afraid the king would recognize him and there might be danger. Finally, he bade Don-grub to wear a mask and tell people his face had been stung by a bee and must keep out of the wind. Thus, the lama took Don-grub into the palace, in the guise of a new disciple.

After they came to the palace, the king was very respectful to the master and his disciple and gave them everything they needed. Four days passed but nobody recognized Don-grub. On the fifth morning, they went with the king for a walk on the roof terrace. At this moment, the princess, carrying ivory and other treasures in her hands, came to offer them to the lama and asked him to bless Prince Don-grub and expiate his sins so that he might quickly ascend to heaven. While saying this, she was nearly choked with sobs.

Suddenly a gust of wind blew the old lama's cap to the ground and Don-grub hastened to pick it up. No sooner did he bend down than his mask fell off. All recognized him to be Don-grub. The princess hugged him and sobbed so hard that the servants, the lama and the king were very moved. Only then did the lama explain in detail Prince Don-grub's history.

King Go-cha said: "So that's what Prince Don-grub is like!" He permitted the princess and Don-grub to marry. Although Prince Don-grub was worried and sad about his younger brother, he could not decline the king's kindness.

On the day of their wedding, everyone in the land, high and low, was bustling with activity and excited, blowing trumpets and hoisting flags. The old lama held a mass, expounding Buddhist teachings. Everyone was in high spirits with the exception of Tri-shod who, with a guilty conscience, did not dare to stay any longer and sneaked into a neighboring country.

Shortly after the marriage of Prince Don-grub and the princess, King Go-cha passed the throne to him and went with the old lama to practice Buddhism. The old lama gave him the religious name Dgar-ba-dpal. Prince Don-grub truly became a king.

Two years later, Don-grub continued to long for his younger brother Don-yod, and his mind was never at ease. Taking many ministers and attendants and all sorts of weapons, dry grain, money and supplies, he departed on a journey, searching in those places where he had passed before. But still he could find no trace. On the way, Don-grub helped people to do many good things, dredging riverbeds, building bridges and houses and giving alms. So people always knew where the king had been.

At this time, some country folk came to report: "There is a strange creature in the mountain with a human-like body covered all over with white hair. It lives with monkeys day in and day out." Don-grub wondered, "Can it be my brother Don-yod, destined to an unfortunate life?" Quickly he asked the country folk where this creature lived. Then he instructed his ministers and attendants to wait there and he himself went with the country folk. Crossing mountains and rivers, they traveled into the heart of a forest. There he saw the human-shaped creature picking fruit from a tree, placing it on a stone slab and calling: "Elder brother Don-grub! Where are you? Elder brother Don-grub, where are you?"

When Don-grub heard his brother's call, he felt as if a needle had stung his heart and could not help shedding tears. He called, "Younger brother Don-yod! I am here, your elder brother is here!"

Don-yod was stunned for a moment and then rushed forward and threw himself into Don-grub's arms. The brothers hugged tightly, choked with sobbing and laughing, unable to tell whether they were happy or sad.

The two returned to the palace and told others their experience of reviving after death. Everyone sighed in sympathy, and the brothers lived very happily together.

Unfortunately, minister Tri-shod, with the hatred that comes from envy, attacked the country in collusion with robbers from elsewhere. Don-grub and Don-yod led their troops against them until Tri-shod's army was utterly routed and fled to the frontier wilderness.

Later, the two brothers, missing their parents very much, returned to their native land, accompanied by their troops, to visit their parents.

King Pa-la-de-va, already advanced in years and believing he had lost his sons, had been grieving. He often shed tears and prayed that his sons would forgive him. He led a dreary, miserable life. When he heard that troops from the northern country were on their way to his kingdom, he was panic-stricken, but he had no army to defend his country.

While he was worrying, he saw that the leaders of the approaching troops were no other than his sons Don-grub and Don-yod, whom he had prayed for and missed every day. Father and sons hugged each other and sobbed bitterly, recounting their experiences of many years. Again they were saddened, but at least they were reunited now, and their grief turned into joy.

Later, King Pa-la-de-va passed on his throne to Don-yod. And Don-grub went back to be king of Go-cha, and the brothers always remained on brotherly and harmonious terms, until their deaths.

PRINCE DRI-MED-KUN-IDAN

This opera is drawn from a story in the Buddhist scriptures. Its former title was "Crown Prince Sudana Sutra," contained in a section of "Vaipulya of Tripltaka." Its plot is virtually the same as that of the opera.

Countless skal-ba ago,[*] in remote, remote times, King Sras-chung-grags-pa ruled a country called Dpal-sde. Under his administration were 3,000 ministers and sixty tribes, as well as Bsam-vphel and other rare treasures. In particular, the treasure Dgos-vdod-vbum-vbyor, emblematic of the country's well-being, had a miraculous function beyond people's expectation. Whoever possessed this treasure immediately had good luck in everything.

The king had a harem of 1,500 including a queen as well as imperial concubines: 500 came from noble and influential families; 500 came from the families of rich merchants and the other 500 were famed for their beauty. Although he had a queen and so many concubines, none bore him a son or a daughter. The king often worried and grieved over this.

One day, the king invited an oracle diviner to tell him how he could have sons and daughters. The diviner explained the oracle inscriptions,

---

* In Buddhist legends, spanning an extraordinarily long period. Imagine a city 40 kilometers square, where mustard seeds were stored. One seed was taken out every three years; when all the seeds had been removed, it was called a skal-ba, that is, "a skal-ba of mustard seeds city."

121

saying: "If Your Majesty worships the triad of the Buddha, the dharma and the sangha above, provides for monks in the middle and gives alms to the poor below, you will certainly have a prince who is the reincarnation of a Bodhisattva."

The king followed his counsel in performing all these acts, and indeed, a short time afterward, an imperial concubine named Skal-idan-bzang-mo became pregnant. She had rid herself of the eight bad qualities of womanhood and possessed various virtues.

One night, Skal-idan-bzang-mo had a fantastic dream, so she went to the king and said to him:

Noble, honorable, benevolent king,
Listen to my narration of what is in my mind,
A dark night comes at the end of a long, long day,
Lying in bed, I at once entered dreamland.
In the dream I saw all the 360 muscles and tendons of my body,
All coiled at the top of my head,
A celestial guardian's golden staff towered on my crown,
That staff was tall and big,
Rising straight into the sky,
Its five-colored rays shone out from four sides in eight directions,
Rainbow and auspicious light in the sky were woven into a huge
　　canopy,
Three thousand conches were blown, ringing melodiously all over
　　the sky.
What good luck this fantastic dream signifies!
Another lucky thing is: I have become pregnant.
This baby has a rather important origin, extraordinary, we may say,
We must have more Buddhist services performed for his benefit!

Having listened to her words, the king was wild with joy, and said to her:

My beloved, virtuous Queen Skal-idan-bzang-mo,

This auspicious dream of yours is so wonderful.

The celestial guardian's staff symbolizes the arrival

    of a ruler in this world,

The rainbow canopy predicts the reincarnation of a Bodhisattva,

The blowing of 3,000 conches forecasts his fame

    will spread far and wide,

My wish has come true at long last in you.

Burn incense, pay homage to the triad of the Buddha,

    the dharma and the sangha,

Let us thus express our devotion!

After nine months and ten days Queen Skal-idan-bzang-mo did give birth to a prince. As soon as he was born, he muttered the six-word philosophical saying "Om-ma-ni-pad-mal-hum" ("Hail to the jewel in the lotus!" equivalent to the Lord's Prayer, especially in Latin, "Our Father, which art in Heaven"). Because this was so strange, he was named Dri-med-kun-idan. Arrangements were made for him to live in Drin-dgar Palace and to study the rites and Buddhist scriptures. In his youth the prince was proficient in writing, counting and the five kinds of learning and had a good command of the Tripitakata. Everybody was moved by his painstaking efforts in his studies.

One day, Prince Dri-med-kun-idan said to the king: "Most of the mortal beings in the world trouble themselves on account of their greed for wealth and treasures, making calculations all day long, submerging themselves in a sea of bitterness because of their consuming avarice. I pity them for such selfishness, such treachery, such cruelty and such stinginess. To free them from their sufferings, would my father, the king, give me the jewels and treasures you have collected for years to distribute among them as alms, so that all the poor in the world can be fed and clothed and satisfy all their wishes?"

When he heard Dri-med-kun-idan's plea, the king was greatly moved and astonished, and said, "Dri-med-kun-idan, you are the person who gives me the greatest satisfaction. I will certainly make you contented. All right! All the wealth and treasures in my possession are at your disposal. You may give them as alms to anybody."

So Prince Dri-med-kun-idan distributed alms in the presence of everybody on the street. Thus, many poor and disabled and those afflicted with poverty and sickness were freed from misery and led a well-fed, well-clothed life.

Unexpectedly, a vicious official, an extremely treacherous, sinister fellow named Stag-ri, went slyly to the king, saying:

My esteemed, noble king,
Listen to what weighs on the humble official's mind:
A king must possess a good store of wealth and treasures,
Only thus can he be respected by commoners everywhere.
Now all the jewels and treasures of my king
    have been squandered away by Dri-med-kun-idan,
A king with empty hands, truly looks unseemly to others.
In order no longer to disperse the country's wealth,
    be quick to get a bride for Dri-med-kun-idan,
So that she may restrict the profligate prince,
And keep our storehouses heaped with gold, silver and jewels.

The king thought these wicked suggestions reasonable. From then on, he sent officials to make careful inquiries everywhere to arrange for the prince's betrothal.

At that time, the king of a neighboring country named Pad-ma-can had a daughter, Smam-sde-bzang-mo. The princess was charming and had a lovely figure. Whoever saw her was fascinated by her beauty, with no exception. Her complexion was as white as snow and her hair as black as lacquer. She had a particularly sweet, gentle temper and was serene and quiet. In her finery, she looked as if a fairy maiden had descended to this world. The fame of such a princess spread with the wind in all directions like the fragrance of sandalwood.

The ministers of the Dpal-sde kingdom informed the king of this princess after some consultation among themselves, and the king decided to win her to be Prince Dri-med-kun-idan's wife. The wedding ceremony and its festivities were beyond description.

After Princess Smam-sde-bzang-mo became the prince's wife, she took meticulous care of him, esteemed and waited upon him as if he were the great lama. One day she said to the prince:

Your heart is as pure as crystal,
It is difficult to estimate how high your learning and attainment are,
Your impressive, dignified manner commands
   people's respect and love,
You, gem of the gems, are king for
"Turning the wheel of the dharma."[*]
I am willing to attend on you at your side at all times,
I am willing to gaze at your radiant countenance at all times.

Prince Dri-med-kun-idan answered the princess with this poetry:

---

[*] In Buddhist legend, king for "Turning the wheel of the dharma" is the supreme ruler of the earthly world.

How resonant is your sweet, melodious singing,
How splendid is your beautiful countenance,
How noble is your pure, spotless heart!
Whenever I see you, I forget all sorrows.
I hope we'll live happily forever,
Wishing our vows and blessings will come true just as we like.

Indeed, they lived together in conjugal affection and had three little princes in succession: the eldest named Legs-idan, the second, Legs-dpal and the youngest Legs-mdzes. The three sons made their life lively and the family lived in perfect harmony and happiness.

One day, when the king, the prince and the ministers were enjoying the beauty of the flowers and plants, feeling carefree and pleasant, thousands of poor commoners thronged at the palace gates. They gazed fixedly at the king, hoping for alms. Each one was pitiful, like sheep waiting to be butchered at a slaughterhouse. Seeing this, Prince Dri-med-kun-idan gave a long sigh, with tears trickling down his face, and hurriedly returned to his own room.

The king came to the prince's palace and asked him:
Dri-med-kun-idan who is able to make magnificent contributions,
Born in a king's family, dressed in silks and brocades,
You do not lack for food or clothing,
Or endure bullying and humiliation,
Why do you frown and look gloomy all day long—
Tell me clearly what makes you sad.

Prince Dri-med-kun-idan said, "Wise king, my father, you have keen insight into everything, even the slightest affairs; listen carefully to what the prince, your son, tells you. Don't you see the people at the palace gate, afflicted with unbearable sufferings? Some are lame, some blind. They experience all hardships. However comfortable my life is, I can't set my mind at ease. With people in an abyss of misery, how can I help feeling dejected?"

The king said, "The commoners lead a miserable life as retribution for their sins in former incarnations. Cause is cause, effect is effect, without deviation. You trouble yourself in vain, only making yourself unhappy. How does this help them?"

The prince said, "The rich are rich and the poor are poor; wealth and poverty go to extremes. With their lack of food and clothing, the commoners look like skeletons. Now, if we could distribute treasures from our storehouse among them, they would be free of poverty—only then will your son's mind be at ease."

The king had always respected Dri-med-kun-idan's opinions, so he consented to open the storehouse to distribute alms widely. This brought poor people from four sides and eight directions to receive the alms. They constantly recited the philosophical saying, "Om-ma-ni-pad-mai-hum," and were grateful to Prince Dri-med-kun-idan. They felt as if he were a Bodhisattva come to this world to save all human creatures.

Shing-khri-tsan-po, king of a hostile country called Phyi-ma-shing-drung, was an evil man who committed all manner of crimes. When he heard that Prince Dri-med-kun-idan of the Dpal-sde kingdom was spreading alms to aid the poor people and had already made a vow that if anyone were in need, he would willingly give him everything, the evil king brought together all his ministers and consulted with them. He said, "Whoever of you could find some way to go to Dpal-sde and get its treasure Dgos-vdod-vbum-vbyor, emblematic of the kingdom's well-being, I would give him half my kingdom! The ministers did not dare to refuse the mission. Unexpectedly, a Brahmin, so old and without even a single tooth of a small pearl's size in his mouth, bragged that he could bring Dgos-vdod-vbum-vbyor back to present it to the king. The old Brahmin gathered his things and left for Dpal-sde that very day.

When the Brahmin came to the palace gate, he sat there shedding tears. With his hand on the gate, a minister asked him: "Old man, where do you live? Why do you come to our place?"

The Brahmin replied: "I, an old man, live in the capital of Phyi-ma-shing-drung; I have come to see Dri-med-kun-idan to beg for alms."

When Prince Dri-med-kun-idan heard the minister's report, he went out in high spirits of the palace to ask the old man: "Honorable old man, you have taken a long journey, crossing countless mountains and rivers. I suppose, old as you are, you must be tired. Tell me quickly what your difficulties are, I will do everything possible to solve them."

The old Brahmin pretended to be sorrowful, and with palms pressed together and shedding tears, he said, "Gods and Buddhas high above, let me, an old man, tell you what weighs upon my mind: Phyi-ma-shing-drung is my native place, all my family depend on our king for their livelihood. Three years ago the king died of a severe illness. The ministers do not provide for me as a human being. I can never eat my fill during the day and can never sleep at ease in the night. My three sons are of bad character and behave like wild beasts. I, an old solitary man, beg and roam here and there. I have heard you are charitable and help all the poor. I have come from many miles away to beg from you a treasure. Wishing the gods and Buddhas in heaven to bless you with peace and prosperity, I will recite the six-word philosophical saying for you all my life, praying happiness will always be with you!

The prince led the old Brahmin into the treasure house and gave him plenty of money and objects.

But who would expect that the old Brahmin had ulterior motives? He said, "I have come a long way, a distance of many miles, not for the sake of becoming well-fed and well-clothed. For myself I want no gem or treasure; I ask you to bestow upon me no other than Dgos-vdod-vbum-vbyor."

When he heard these words, the prince was shocked and said, "Honorable old man, pray listen to my explanation, I cannot give away the treasure emblematic of our kingdom's well-being. If my father, the king, found out, it might annoy him and turn him against me. I cannot give it to you because I do not have the right."

The old Brahmin looked sullen, saying:

Loud thunder but small raindrops, what you have said is just lies!

You do not deserve your reputation of being charitable and fond of
    giving alms.

I have come to you across countless miles—

Who would expect you to be a miser?

A horse without a saddle is unfit for riding,

A dish not flavored with salt is not palatable,

One who does not keep his promise
    cannot be counted among men.

I do not want any other treasure,

Let me say farewell and leave for home.

Prince Dri-med felt perplexed, hesitating for a while. Finally, he made up his mind to give him the treasure as alms, warning the old man: "This treasure is unusual. The old dragon king in the sea had given it to the Bodhisattva of Immeasurable Splendor, who in turn gave it to my father, the king. With this treasure, our country is insured good weather for crops, can defeat the troops of any enemy country and ensure peace for people, high and low, across the land. Now, at the risk of my life and punishment from my father, the king, I'll give it to you as alms." The prince also gave him an elephant and told the old Brahmin to leave on elephant-back in haste. "If you delay, my father, the king, may hear of this and not allow you to leave." Of course, the old Brahmin rode off on the elephant, carrying the treasure, and rushed straight to Phyi-ma-shing-drung to boast of his outstanding service.

When the vicious minister, Stag-ri, learned what had happened, he hastened to the king and said, "Your Majesty, something disastrous has occurred; the prince has made overwhelming trouble. He gave the treasure emblematic of our kingdom's well-being to the enemy country! Dri-med committed such an outrage! What will come next if you do not punish him?"

Hearing this, the king was panic-stricken and hurriedly called Dri-med to him, inquiring: "Dri-med, my son, you must tell the truth! Have you presented the treasure emblematic of our country's well-being as gift to others?"

Dri-med, with his palms pressed together, made a bow and kept silent. After repeated urging by the king, he finally said, "The day before yesterday came an old Brahmin from the capital of distant Phyi-ma-shing-drung. He was dark complexioned and dressed in rags. What he told me really aroused my sympathy, and he kept begging for the treasure emblematic of our country's well-being. To satisfy him, I presented the treasure to this man."

The king was so upset that he fainted away. He regained his consciousness after a long while and scolded the prince for giving the enemy the treasure of the country's well-being, without permission.

The prince explained that everything he did was to make others happy and contented. He would willingly give others even his own life, his wife and children as alms. He also said:

Bees are busy all day long, flying here and there
    to gather flowers and make honey,
Laying down their own lives and going to the king
    of hell at long last.
A miser who has accumulated riches
    cannot take one penny into the nether world after his death;
A king should think constantly of his commoners,
He should purge himself of greed early.

The king was extremely angry and ordered warriors to tie the prince with ropes and lead him out of the palace, parading with all his clothes stripped off through the thronging streets.

The princess Smam-sde-bzang-mo was also led into the crowd, because of her connection with the prince. She had never experienced such suffering and, disheveled, lamenting to heaven and knocking her head on the earth, complained of her grievances and prayed to the gods and Buddhas for protection. Prince Dri-med was calm and advised her to be quiet. By day, they were led by warriors and paraded through the city, and by night they were imprisoned in a mountain cave.

The king brought together all the ministers and consulted with them on how to punish Dri-med-kun-idan.

Some said: "He should be skinned."

Some said: "His limbs should be cut off."

Some said: "His heart and liver should be cut out."

Some said: "His eyes should be gouged out."

Some said: "He should be beheaded."

Some said: "He should be bombarded by cannon."

Some said: "His head should be hung over the palace gate."

Some said: "He should be thrown alive into a snake den."

At this time, an honest, faithful old minister named Zla-ba-bzang-po, a devotee of Buddhism, said: "The ministers said wanton words and were perverse in their behavior. If the prince were killed, who would become the king in the future? Prince Dri-med-kun-idan is so open and generous he never thinks of his own interests. Now he is led naked into the street, and feels so ashamed to be gazed at by people! This is our country's shame and humiliation. All the commoners are talking about it! Is it against the law to aid the poor and the afflicted? Why do you not promptly set the prince free?"

So the king ordered the warriors to lead the prince and his wife in front of the throne, and said to them, "I forgive you. It is because you are young and ignorant that you have committed such foolish errors, exhausting the storehouse and dispersing treasures. Now I exile you to the desolate mountain Ha-shang-ri-bo. You must mend your ways and make a fresh start."

Prince Dri-med-kun-idan accepted these orders and prayed that others would not experience the same suffering as he had, and then returned to his palace to get ready for exile to the mountain Ha-shang-ri-bo. All loyal, upright ministers, commoners and tribal chieftains came to present gifts, some giving gold, silver and jewels, and some giving horses and elephants. But when the gifts came into Dri-med-kun-idan's hands, he at once gave them as alms to the poor. He said to Princess Smam-sde-bzang-mo, "My lifelong partner, pray listen to me. You need not worry for my sake, I'll go alone to the wilderness and live there quietly for twelve years. You may return to your parents' home with the three children, and wait there for our reunion as husband and wife."

But Princess Smam-sde-bzang-mo said, "My prince on whom I always rely, how can I let you go alone to Ha-shang? How can you send me and the children to my parents' home? How can we, husband and wife, father and children, go to separate places? It is not wrong for husband and wife to share only peace and happiness and not suffering. My prince, you must not go into wild flights of fancy. Pray take me and our sons with you to Ha-shang."

The prince said, "Smam-sde-bzang-mo, you must think over this problem carefully: Exile cannot be compared with living in our native place. First, you have no parents to look after you; second, you have no nectar or other delicious drink. When you are hungry, you can eat only wild fruit as grain. When thirsty, you can drink only snow as wine, sew up leaves as clothes, sleep on a straw cushion, in wind, rain, snow and frost, day and night throughout the seasons. Not even birds and animals will be your companions. Is it necessary for you to experience such hardships?"

But the princess insisted on going along with him. The prince had to yield to her request and promised to go with her and their sons to the mountain Ha-shang-ri-bo. But he warned her if somebody begged for her as alms, he would probably give her and their sons away, to keep his former pledge.

When Prince Dri-med-kun-idan went to say farewell to his mother, the queen was reluctant to let her son go so far away, but she dared not disobey the king's order, which was as firm as iron. She could only shed tears and bless them:

Gods and Buddhas who have power over all directions,
Bodhisattvas who have great supernatural strength,
Four celestial guardians in protection of all mankind,
Please listen to a woman's prayer,

My son will be exiled to Ha-shang,

Pray protect him keeping him safe and happy.

Level rugged paths, do away with barriers,

Turn high mountain into plains to reduce his hardships,

Let wild fruit on desolate mountain become delicious food,

Let flowing water in the river valley become sweet, fragrant wine,

Let leaves become colorful embroidered brocade,

Let straw cushion become soft lotus flower bed.

Let the roaring of lions and tigers and the crying of the monkeys
    become the preachings of the Great Vehicle Buddhism,

Let rushing cataracts and murmuring streams become melodious
    celestial music, pleasant and relaxing,

Let sultry heat become a refreshing breeze,

Turn diseases and disasters into health and strength.

Wishing the gods in the unseen world may protect him,

May my son return to his native place and reunite with me!

Then Prince Dri-med-kun-idan, Princess Smam-sde-bzang-mo and
the three little princes rode in two carriages straight for Ha-shang-ri-bo
in the north, with their luggage and utensils loaded on two elephants.
At their departure, the queen said to her son, shedding tears while
clasping his hands:

My son! You are mother's heart and liver,

Cut off and thrown to the distant, desolate mountain,

My mind is like the setting sun,

It can never forget my son's suffering.

Between spring and summer when the thunder first claps,

Mother will call your pet name three times;

In autumn and winter when the chill wind comes,

Mother will call your pet name three times;

When the cuckoo cries pathetically in the sky,

Mother will call your pet name three times;

My son! When you miss your mother very much,

You may call my name three times,

Let the hearts of mother and son be linked!

Mother and son parted, shedding tears, and the prince departed with his wife and the three children.

Along the way, they met five poor people, begging for alms. The prince gave them the carriages, horses, elephants and utensils. Then, with the prince leading the children and the princess carrying the grain, they walked on foot towards Ha-shang-ri-bo. On the way they saw flowers and wild grass all over the hill and water flowing in the streams, but they saw no human being, only wild beasts running here and there. The princess felt melancholy, and the prince advised her better to go back quickly to the palace. He warned that more hardships lay ahead and he was afraid she might not be able to bear them. But even so, the princess did not consent to go back alone. When they came to a pretty spot with a beautiful mountain and stream, a dense forest and chirping birds and fragrant flowers blooming, the princess advised the prince to settle there. He refused, saying that their destination was Ha-shang and they must not linger halfway in a land of comfort and happiness.

Facing countless hardships on the way, they came to a place where they met three Brahmins begging for alms. The prince said: "Apart from my wife and children, I have nothing to offer you." The three Brahmins said, "Pray give us your three children as alms." The prince said, "My three children are too young and have never left their

135

mother. Maybe it would be better to let their mother go along with you and spare them the grief of separation."

Then, remembering his former pledge to satisfy others' wishes and grant whatever is requested, he told the princess to go and gather wild fruit on the hill to entertain the guests. After she had left, he gave his three children to the three Brahmins.

The children sobbed bitterly and even the prince could not help weeping. When the princess came back after gathering some wild fruit, she saw both her children and the Brahmins gone, and she knew they had been given as alms to the Brahmins. She was as grief-stricken as if a knife had stabbed her to the heart and lay on the ground, weeping with deep sorrow:

Three clever quick-witted children,
Given as alms to greedy, fierce Brahmins,
Just like thriving, luxuriant crops,
Hit by hailstones with nothing left.
Gods and Buddhas in the heaven!
Lamas on the earth!
My three children are like the tip of my heart,
Why are they cut off alive?
What grief for us to part forever,
Can it be that you Brahmins do not pity us a tiny bit?

She wept so bitterly that the sky darkened, everything was dim, and she fainted away. The prince revived her and urged her not to be sad because he had to fulfill his earlier vow. Moreover, sacrificing one's own interests for the benefit of others was most noble. With these words he himself shed tears too.

The prince and his wife continued their journey. At this time,

Lha-brgya-byin and Lha-tshangs-pa,* disguising themselves as two Brahmins, came to the prince to beg for alms, saying, "Prince Dri-med-kun-idan, your fame spreads far and wide. We are short of servants and beset with difficulties in everything. Pray give your princess as alms to the two of us!"

The prince consoled her for a while and then steeled his heart and gave the princess to the men. But Lha-brgya-byin and Lha-tshangs-pa so much admired Prince Dri-med-kun-idan's generosity that they returned the princess to him, transforming themselves into a rainbow and vanishing into the skies.

The couple continued to walk for a long distance. On the bank of a broad river they came to a large city which Lha-tshangs-pa had used his supernatural power to conjure up, and the prince and his wife were invited to stay there for seven days. Lha-tshangs-pa, transforming himself into a boy, came to wait upon them and advised them to stay on permanently, saying it was unnecessary to go to the desolate mountain of Ha-shang.

But the prince was unwilling to linger in the comfortable life and insisted on going to his destination. On the way they continued to encounter many frightening, horrible things: wild beasts roaring, poisonous water gurgling like a boiling cauldron, devils and demons with long, sharp, protruding teeth—but none of these could harm them. At long last, they arrived at the desolate mountain of Ha-shang. The peak was snow-capped and the mountain was girdled with cataracts half-way up.

As the prince arrived, leaves grew on the withered trees of the desolate mountain, withered grass became verdant again and flowers

---

* Two Buddhist gods.

blossomed all over the barren ground. Tigers, leopards, wolves, bears, elephants, yaks, egrets, geese, peacocks and cuckoos, as well as celestial dragons, yakshas (malevolent spirits), celestial musicians, and devils and demons stood in a procession to welcome them.

After that, the desolate mountain changed its countenance, becoming a scenic spot with murmuring streams, flocks of birds and herds of animals, trees laden with fruit and flowers and grass in a riot of colors. The prince built a cottage with twigs and leaves and lived in it in quiet meditation for twelve years.

At that time, the princess missed her children very much and prayed beside a large river:

Water that flows past Dpal-sde kingdom,
Greet my three children when you meet them,
Tell them their parents are in good health,
And only miss the three of them.
Our hearts are laden with sorrow like a knife stabbing at us,
We cannot bear this forever,
Twelve years have flitted away,
In wishing parents and sons be reunited and no longer separated.

Surging water flowed through thousands of streams and their tributaries and finally conveyed these words to the ears of the three children. Hearing them, all three shouted their parents' names and, climbing to a peak, they gazed northward. Just then, a nightingale flew past and the youngest prince, Legs-mdzes, prayed, saying:

Nightingale flies to a place of joy,
All people love to listen to your singing,
But your melodious music reminds us brothers of our grief.
In your flight to the north,
When you pass the desolate mountain Ha-shang,

Where live my father and mother,
Pray tell them we brothers are in good health.
Only the sorrow of missing our parents torments
    our hearts at all times.
Our parents, pray pity your sons' sufferings,
Return to our native place soon!

The nightingale flew across thousands of mountain peaks to the mountain Ha-shang and conveyed the prayer of the three sons to Prince Dri-med. When they heard the bird, the couple were moved to tears, which streamed down all over their faces, and they decided to go back home. The birds and animals on the mountain were reluctant to part with them and stood in a procession to see them off.

On their return journey, the couple came to the place called Stod-lung-nas, where they met a blind Brahmin who extended his hand to beg alms from the prince. The prince said: "I have given away everything I have, what do you want?"

The blind Brahmin said: "I request you to give me your pair of eyes as alms?" Without hesitation, the prince gouged out his eyes, gave them as alms to the beggar and placed them in his eye sockets. The blind Brahmin's eyes brightened at once and he saw everything clearly. The Brahmin kowtowed to express his gratitude to the prince and then rushed back to Dpal-sde kingdom. All the people were astonished to see that the blind man had recovered his eyesight. He told them that Prince Dri-med-kun-idan had given his eyes as alms.

At this moment the king heard this news and hastened to send minister Zla-ba-bzang-po with some attendants to welcome the prince home. When the minister arrived at Ha-shang, he found the prince, blind and exhausted, and the princess' tears streaming down her face.

Zla-ba-bzang-po felt very sad. But the prince, learning that Zla-ba-bzang-po had come to welcome him back, felt overjoyed and asked him, while stroking his head, "Loyal and upright Zla-ba-bzang-po, have you had a pleasant journey? Is the state power of the Dpal-sde kingdom secure? Do the people enjoy a peaceful and prosperous life? Are my parents in good health?"

Seeing the prince's affliction, Zla-ba-bzang-po was choked with sobbing. The prince prayed in silence: "To relieve the suffering of Zla-ba-bzang-po and Princess Smam-sde-bzang-mo, pray the gods and the Buddhas bless me and let me regain my eyesight!" Sure enough, his eyes recovered their sight and former appearance. Together, the three of them traveled to the kingdom of Dpal-sde.

They passed the Phyi-ma-shing-drung on their way, where King Shing-khri-tsan-po came from a great distance to welcome them. The king deeply repented his conduct. The three Brahmins brought back the three little princes and expressed their thanks. Dri-med-kun-idan invited the three Brahmins to go to the Dpal-sde kingdom and promised to give them money and other things as alms.

When Prince Dri-med-kun-idan arrived at the gate of the kingdom, ministers and commoners throughout the country came from far and wide to welcome him, and the king burned incense in welcome.

Dpal-sde streets and lanes resounded with the beating of gongs and drums and were decorated with many flags and pennants. People everywhere in the land, high and low, were jubilant. Later, the king abdicated the throne and Prince Dri-med-kun-idan inherited it. Everyone all over the country was bathed in benevolence and kindness, nearly all their desires and dreams came true, and they led a happy, contented life ever after.

MAIDEN SNANG-SA

The opera was adapted from a story believed to be true. Judging by the preface to the manuscript, ballad singers first adapted it to be narrated and sung before it was transplanted into the Tibetan opera for performance.

In the vast snow land of Tibet there is a village called "Rgyang-vpher-knug" where an ordinary family lived. The man's name was Kun-bzang-bde-chen and his wife was Nyang-tsha-gsal-sgron. They were law-abiding vegetarians and devotees of Buddhism.

One night, the woman had a fantastic dream and, after waking up, she was greatly astonished and did not dare tell others. She had the same fantastic dream for several nights in succession and finally could no longer keep the secret to herself. So she said to her husband:

My respected head of the family,

I want to tell you something that is weighing upon my mind,

For three nights in succession I did not have a quiet sleep;

I dreamed that I arrived at a fantastic place,

With white jade on the ground, shining radiantly,

And blocks of gold, inlaid with mother-of-pearl,

Resembling the paradise of the deities.

Golden rays illuminated my lap,

A lotus flower sprang up, sending forth its fragrance in all

   directions.

Golden-colored bees resemble clouds,

Butterflies of green jade color look like rain,

Buzzing, flying, whirling and clamoring.

I was both joyful and frightened.

What did this fantastic dream predict, bad luck and danger?

Or was it a sign of good luck?

After listening to his wife's narration, the man said to her:

My beautiful life companion,

Listen to my explanation:

A dream is just a dream, not real; don't be frightened.

Recall the deity's rays shone on your lap,

A lotus flower grew up in your lap;

It sent forth refreshing fragrance,

Bees and butterflies flew to and fro.

Recall when we were young and had pearl-white teeth,

You did not give birth to a son;

Now we are old and white-haired,

You'll give birth to a daughter, even better than a son.

Let's go promptly to pay homage to Buddha,

And let's be quick to thank heaven....

The couple were very joyful and even more devout than before in their Buddhist practices. They worshipped Buddhist teachings and Triratna (the triad of the Buddha, the dharma and the sangha). Untiringly, they gave alms to the poor and they gave donations to the lamas in the monasteries. A short time later, the wife did become pregnant and in the first ten days of the monkey month of the horse year (precisely the tenth day of the gathering of goddesses, on a Thursday when meteors illuminated the sky), she gave birth to a daughter who was named Snang-sa, meaning "rosy clouds of a hundred thousand rays."

The girl grew very rapidly. In one month she was bigger than year-old children of other families. She grew as much in a day as other children grew in one month. She had an extraordinarily gentle temper. Her beauty was unusual because it was the beauty of all people of the world. Gazing at her was pleasing to the eye. The singing of cuckoos, nightingales and larks is sweet and melodious but could not compare with her voice, which had a joyful sound. Her father often said happily, "Who would have thought a donkey could give birth to a robust, vigorous mule and a yak could give birth to a fat, strong bull-yak offspring? We, a rustic old couple, couldn't have thought we would bear a beautiful maiden. We should, indeed, thank heaven!"

The maiden was not only beautiful and gentle but was also a good worker. She was expert and industrious in every job such as roasting highland barley, weaving *phrug* (a woolen fabric), and doing farm work. Indeed, her family became more prosperous with each passing day.

At the age of fifteen, Maiden Snang-sa was known throughout Tibet. Young men came as her suitors in a continuous stream from eastern Tibet, western Tibet and the region between eastern Tibet and Qamdo. But none of them could win her. She was still young and reluctant to part from her parents, and her parents cherished her as treasure more precious than a hundred sons and were unwilling to let her depart from them.

At this time, there was a chieftain named Grags-chen-pa in Nyang-stod, in western Tibet. He possessed land, manors and pasture in an area about 500 kilometers around. His wife had died, leaving behind a son named Grags-pa-bsam-grub and a daughter named Sne-mo-ne-gtso. The chieftain wanted to find a suitable wife for his son, and made inquiries everywhere and tried a hundred and one ways to achieve this purpose.

That year, there gathered at the fair at Gnas-rnying Monastery in Rgyal-rtse everybody from white-haired elders to children with milk teeth, lamas in yellow robes and common folk in gray clothes. Naturally, Chieftain Grags-chen-pa also came for the festivities, with his attendants.

Maiden Snang-sa also attended the fair, and her parents hoped their daughter would win the praise of all the people there. They dressed her as beautifully as they could, and she was by nature a maiden of exceptional charm. That day she looked so lovely: Her face resembled the bright, clear moon and her glossy hair was like the soft young shoots of a special willow tree. Truly, she was as beautiful as a lotus flower floating on the water, a peacock turning on a lawn, a bright lantern shining in a crowd and a goddess descending to this world. Escorted by her girl companion, Vdzoms-pa-skyil, she lit the lantern, paid homage and attended dances and operas at the fair.

As Chieftain Grags-chen-pa was walking through a winding corridor, he looked out of the window and saw maiden Snang-sa. From that moment, he could not take his eyes off her. So he instructed his trusted attendant Bsod-nams-dpal-dkyil to seize Snang-sa from the crowd, like a hawk would seize a sparrow, a hound would seize a rabbit, or a cat would catch a mouse. He brought her into the chieftain's presence. Grags-chen-pa snatched at the maiden's clothing with his left hand and raised a cup of wine in his right hand, saying: "Maiden with a beautiful figure, maiden with a pleasant voice, maiden with a sweet fragrance, is it possible that you are the daughter of a goddess?

Is it possible that you are the daughter of a deva musician? Where do
you actually come from? What is your father's name? How is your
mother called? What is your own name? Tell me the truth! I am the
chieftain of Rgyak-rtse in Nyang-stod; my name Grags-chen-pa, like
a thunderclap, is known far and near. Perhaps it is impossible that you
do not know this.

"My son Grags-pa-bsam-grub, already eighteen years old, is still
unmarried. He is the jewel of my heart. I want to take you back as my
daughter-in-law to live with my son in married bliss until you are old."

The maiden finally began to understand, and said, "Honorable
chieftain, headman whose fame spreads far and wide, I am a native
of Rgyang-vpher-knug in Rgyal-rtse. My father is Kun-bzang-bde-
chen and my mother Nyang-tsha-gsal-sgron. My childhood name is
Snang-sa-vod-vbum. Please consider the matter. I am from an ordinary
family. How can I marry into an important family? Although a pine
tree is green and luxuriant, it cannot be used as a decoration on a table.
Although marble is smooth and lustrous, it cannot match green jade.
Although a lark can soar in the skies, it cannot become the friend of
a hawk. Although the maiden of an ordinary family is beautiful and
charming, she cannot be the daughter-in-law of an official. Please
allow me to return home."

The chieftain's attendant, Bsod-nams-dpal-dkyil, brought forward
a piece of lustrous jade and tied it with red silk and many-colored silk
threads. He handed it to the chieftain, saying:

Unhappy at heart, pretending to be joyful and in high spirits,
A young man is recruited into the army to fight far away;
Happy at heart but pretending to be displeased,
A maiden hears someone give her an offer of marriage.
First, put this betrothal gift on the maiden's head,

Most of the affair has been settled.

The chieftain added the following words:
Disobeying a high official's instructions,
A clever person becomes a fool.
Disobeying a headman's words,
Misfortune will come at once.
The sun hangs high in the sky,
A lotus flower grows low on the ground;
Although high and low differ,
They may become good friends all the same.
An arrow is long, a bow short,
Long and short differ,
But they may become good friends all the same;
Seas and oceans are large, fish and shrimp small,
Large and small differ,
They may become good friends all the same;
A high official is noble, a peasant girl low,
Noble and low differ,
They may become related in marriage and friendship all the same.

Then he pinned the jade on the maiden Snang-sa's head without
asking for her consent and, turning to those present, said:
Listen, all people here:
Beginning today, the son of Chieftain Grags-chen-pa of Nyang-stod
    has taken maiden Snang-sa as his wife.
An influential family cannot snatch her away,
An insignificant family cannot steal her away;
A family in between cannot take her as daughter-in-law.

Flying high, she cannot soar into the sky,

Plunging low, she cannot go deep into the ground.

All of you have seen.

Maiden Snang-sa belongs to Chieftain Grags-chen-pa's family.

The chieftain and his company went away in an uproar. People attending the festivities left the fair, sighing. Maiden Snang-sa and her girl companion Vdzoms-pa-skyi were silent and gloomy all the way home.

After returning home, she did not dare tell her parents about how the chieftain had forced her to marry his son. She hid the fact, deciding to wait and see what would happen.

A few days later, the chieftain arrived, bringing fine wine, clothing and jewels for the marriage ceremony. He brought a sum of money for the bride's family, in accordance with Tibetan custom. Going right to the door of Snang-sa's home, the chieftain's party knocked. The maiden's mother saw them through the window and said to the father, "Chieftain Grags-chen-pa has come to the door of our home. Be quick and welcome him in."

But Snang-sa's father said, with a sorrowful face, "The chieftain never comes to a village for nothing. When he arrives at the door of any family, it is as if an owl has perched on the roof. Who knows what disaster will occur? We must try to deal with him properly. It would be better for you women to receive him."

The mother opened the door to greet the chieftain, holding up the *hata* (a piece of silk used as a greeting gift among the Tibetans) with both hands. When he had come in, he told her in detail of the family's offer of marriage to her daughter. The simple woman rejoiced inwardly, seeing that the influential chieftain condescended to ask her consent for his family's offer of marriage. She hastened to call Snang-sa's father, who had no choice but to give his consent.

The chieftain ordered his attendants to present as wedding gifts the fine wine, clothing and jewels, and the sum of money to repay the maiden's family for bringing her up. Then, turning, he said to the maiden herself: "Maiden, at the Gnas-rnying-zung-drug fair, you looked like the moon rising from the eastern hill in India. Why didn't you tell your family about our meeting? Why do you behave so awkwardly when a guest comes?"

But the maiden kept silent and reserved. Turning to Snang-sa's parents, the chieftain said:

Beginning today,
Maiden Snang-sa belongs to our family,
Say not she has been seized by a high official,
Say not she has been cheated and brought away by a rascal;
Say not she soars up into the sky;
Say not she has gone deep into the ground;
Say not you parents do not allow her to part from you;
Say not the maiden is unwilling to leave her home.
Today, tomorrow,
The day after tomorrow will be a day of good luck,
I shall send five hundred people to welcome her
    for a wedding ceremony.
Hurry up, make good preparations.

Her mother advised Snang-sa to marry willingly into the chieftain's family because they had plenty of gold and silver and a splendid house. But the maiden was disgusted with her mother's words and said to her:

Separation will be the result of this meeting.

I am unwilling to marry into his family;

Poverty comes at the end of wealth and rank;

I do not like his family's gold and silver heaped into a mountain;

A house will crumble in the end,

I do not like his family's many-storied mansion.

I will not go! Please, Mama!

The maiden's father sighed in despair: "Grags-chen-pa is well known to be a vicious man. He is more raging than fire and more devastating than water. If you refuse to go, and offend him, your mother and I might lose our lives."

Two days later, emissaries came to escort the maiden to the wedding ceremony and she had to array herself in finery. At the time of her departure her father and mother advised her:

My daughter, you are superior to a son.

You are leaving father and mother for another's family,

In the morning you must get up earlier than the cock,

At night you must go to bed later than an old dog;

The dowry father and mother give you is highland barley, wheat and green pea,

Silks, satins, Tibetan woolens and blankets,

Gold, silver, jade, jadeite and pearls.

Be careful in everything because you will be alone and far from home.

Snang-sa had been married into the chieftain's family for seven years and given birth to a son named Lhavu-ar-po. She had truly cast away the ten evils and possessed the eight virtues. Everyone in the family, high and low, old and young, respected her, liked her and was on intimate terms with her. The chieftain even intended to turn over the keys of all the 64 storehouses and assign her to take charge of them. But someone was irritated by this, her younger sister-in-law, Sne-mo-ne-gtso, who had always supervised household affairs herself. Even trifles could not be done without Sne-mo-ne-gtso's decision. Seeing that Snang-sa won the ever-growing favor of the family, Sne-mo-ne-gtso was very resentful and tried to get others to dislike Snang-sa. She sowed discord, spread rumors and slanders and made Snang-sa eat coarse grain and wear rags.

Snang-sa was unwilling to tell her husband about all this, nor did she want to tell the chieftain lest it would cause discord in the family. So she suffered alone.

She often hugged her son and said, "Without you, my lifeblood that brought me so much tenderness, I would have become a nun or returned to my maiden home long ago."

One day, carrying her son on her back, Snang-sa went to the garden to seek ease from her cares. By chance, she met her husband, Grags-pa-bsam-grub, who was there washing his hair. She hastened to help him rinse it. Then he laid his head on her bosom and, as she combed his hair, she saw that the flowers in the garden were withered by autumn frost and only a few still fluttering in the wind. She felt the scene was like her own sorrow and could not help shedding tears.

The tears dripped on her husband's chest and awakened him. When he saw Snang-sa's face stained with tears, she could no longer conceal her sadness, and said to him:

"I am kindhearted to my sister-in-law, but she is as malicious to me as a knife. She repays my kindness with vicious deeds. I lend her wine and she returns me water. When I keep silent, she says I am a fool;

when I say a few words, she says I am a lunatic. When I walk outside, she says I am a coquette; when I sit at home, she says I am blind. My parents are far away in my native village; who will listen when I tell my innermost thoughts?"

After listening to his wife's words, Grags-pa-bsam-grub pondered a while and then said, "It is true you miss your parents. Together we shall visit them in a few days. It may also be true my sister has mistreated you. I can admonish her."

A short time afterwards, the season came for harvesting highland barley. The whole family went to the fields to harvest the crop, under the supervision of the sister-in-law, Sne-mo-ne-gtso.

At that time, the lamas left their monasteries and went down in all directions to gather alms. One of them came with his disciple from Ding-ri Mountain into Snang-sa's presence to beg. He murmured:

Pay homage to the Buddha, Buddhist teachings and monks,

Freed from the six ways of transmigration.

You give us alms,

We expound Buddhist doctrine and teachings to you.

Your beautiful body

Resembles a colorful rainbow on eastern grasslands;

The rainbow is radiant but cannot last.

Your beautiful body

Resembles a cuckoo in the southern woods,

The cuckoo sings melodiously, but cannot last long.

Your beautiful body

Resembles a dragon princess in the western sea,

The dragon princess leads a luxurious life but cannot live forever.

Your beautiful body

Resembles a thunderbolt in the northern wilderness;

The thunderbolt sounds loud and clear but cannot last long.
Your beautiful body
Resembles a mural in the central Buddha-worshipping hall;
Murals are beautiful and bright-colored but cannot last long.
Once the god of death falls on your head,
You cannot resist him, despite your infinite strength;
You cannot hide from him, despite your mouselike cowardice;
You cannot deceive him, despite your high-sounding words;
You cannot bribe him with gold, silver or wealth;
You cannot block his way despite your high rank;
You cannot be spared despite thousands of entreaties;
You cannot escape even though you are a fleetfooted runner.
Remember, never return empty handed from treasure mountain
Hasten to believe in Buddhism; it is never wrong to give alms.

After Snang-sa had heard the ballad, boundless devotion sprang up in her heart and she wanted very much to give alms to the lama. But she had no right over the family's possessions, and had to say: "Two reverend lamas, although I am willing to give alms, I have no power to do so. The maiden over there is in charge of our household affairs. Pray beg alms from her!"

The two lamas turned, approached the sister-in-law and sang the ballad again. To their surprise, the sister-in-law let loose a torrent of abuse:

"You two beggars, what are you doing here? In the summer, you beg for something white, milk, butter and cheese. In the winter, you beg for something sour, Tibetan wine. When you are in the mountains, you do not sit in meditation and recite sutras. When you are in the fields, you do not work in earnest. When you see whatever can be seized, you become robbers. When you see whatever can be stolen, you become thieves. All day long you do no other than telling lies, bragging, cheating and intimidating others. I will give you no alms. Go to that woman Snang-sa, daughter-in-law of the chieftain, who is more attractive than a peacock, with a voice more melodious than cuckoo and a face more radiant and beautiful than rainbow and power more mighty than a mountain. I am only her servant and have no right to give alms."

The two lamas had to go back to Snang-sa and told her what Sne-mo-ne-gtso had just said. Snang-sa became so angry that she could not utter a word. She mustered all her courage and measured out alms for the lamas. They thanked her again and again and told her they studied under Saint Mila-raspa. Seeing that they were the disciples of a saint, she measured three more khals of highland barley for them. She also kowtowed and paid homage to them. The two lamas recited one volume of sutras for her blessing and then returned to the mountain.

The sister-in-law saw all these circumstances and the flames of her anger spurted up thirty feet high. She rolled up her sleeves and raised her fists. With a wooden club in her hands, she came to Snang-sa and scolded her: "You spendthrift woman, pretty outside but filthy inside! There are thousands of beggars in front and behind the mountain, uphill and downhill. How can you give alms to all of them? I'm afraid you'll give yourself away too!"

Snang-sa tried to smile and explained, "Ancient people said: 'When a beggar says something malicious or an old crow holds stinking meat in its mouth, it will cause unrest all over the mountain and the valley.' I was afraid that their clamor would damage the reputation of the chieftain's family. If we give alms to the poor and do homage to the Buddha and the monks, it is using our wealth properly. Bees collect honey into a heap to benefit others. Please do not regard lamas as beggars, and I am not a spendthrift either."

Sister-in-law Sne-mo-ne-gtso did not listen to Snang-sa's words. Instead she spread the word that Snang-sa had been attracted by the lamas' handsome looks and sweet words and flirted with them, making the chieftain's family lose face. Without allowing her to plead innocence, the sister-in-law cuffed and kicked her, pushed and shoved her and pulled off a skein of her hair. She rushed to her brother and wept, saying:

Hateful is Snang-sa the damned woman,
Her behavior is indecent
I told her to reap the crops but she didn't work well,
She spent all her time doing filthy and improper things.
When the sun rose this morning,
There came two young men,
They came to the fields for no other reason,
Than to flirt with Snang-sa;
I gave her good advice,
She refused to listen, as if a spring breeze swept past her ears.
Then, out of shame, she flew into a rage,
And pulled off a lot of my hair.
Brother, keep in mind that we were born of the same parents,
Punish this demon severely on my behalf.

When Grags-pa-bsam-grub heard his sister's story, he rushed off to look for Snang-sa without considering the rights and wrongs of the case. At a corner of the field he saw her sobbing. Rushing forward at once, he scolded her:

When a dog begging for food is tied on the roof,

it barks furiously at the stars in the sky;
When an earthen jar is baked in the sun,
    its base curls up higher than its mouth;
When a donkey is well-fed with fodder,
    it can kick and hurt a good horse;
If a boatman is not acquainted with the currents of a river,
    the boat will be pierced through by shoals;
When a beggar is acquainted with the temper of dogs,
    he will carry the beat-dog club on his shoulder;
You, contemptible woman, not appreciating my favors,
    dare behave so indecently!

These words pierced her heart like sharp arrows. She felt so wronged and broken-hearted that she could not speak. Her husband became more angry when he saw her speechless and thought his sister's words were true. He stepped forward, pulled her hair and dragged her around, cuffing and kicking her. He beat her so hard that not a single spot on her body remained unscathed and she suffered three broken ribs. Snang-sa was almost at the point of death.

Luckily, men and women servants felt sorry for her and tried to intervene. They pulled Grags-pa-bsam-grub away and took Snang-sa to her room, where she stayed alone and grieved, hugging her son Lhavu-dar-po.

At this time, Sha-kya-rgyal-mtshan, senior lama in Skyid-po-yar-klung Monastery, knew that Snang-sa-vod-vbum had suffered a great disaster. He transformed himself into a handsome young man and led a monkey at his side, begging for alms while the monkey performed. He went to the base of the many-storied building where Snang-sa lived and began to sing an opera, with the monkey performing. Every line in the opera advised people to abandon evil deeds, follow Buddhist training and receive good rewards for their good deeds. This message appealed to Snang-sa.

As Lhavu-dar-po was a child, he was drawn by the monkey's antics. Mother and son gazed down at the performance for a long time. She was very moved and intended to give some money to the man begging, but she had no part of the family's possessions. So she called the young man into her room and, taking out some jewels from her dowry, gave them to him. She also told him that she was unwilling to live there any longer and was determined to go into the hills to take up strict Buddhist training. She said, "My husband is my life partner but he is like a banner on a flagstaff, fluttering with the wind. He believes other people's words and beats his wife. Although my son is very good, he is still young and understands little. I can no longer put up with my sister-in-law, who is vicious, wicked and crafty.

"You have roamed across the land – pray tell me which mountain is the quietest, which temple has eminent monks, which lama possesses great supernatural power and which living Buddha has the most profound Buddhist attainment?"

The beggar said: "I've traveled all over the land and never told a lie. Going northward, you'll find a famous ancient temple at the foot of a mountain that looks like a reclining bullock and the mountain behind it resembles a lion gazing up at the sky. Skyid-po-yar-klung is the name of the temple and Sha-kya-rgyal-mtshan is a lama with great supernatural power. If you sincerely wish to practice Buddhism, you may go to him for help."

Snang-sa's heart rejoiced. She took out five corals and three turquoises and gave them as alms to the beggar.

At that time, Chieftain Grags-chen-pa was supervising the workers in the fields from a tall ladder. Because he was up high, he heard a man and a woman talking in Snang-sa's room. He recognized Snang-sa's voice but the man's voice was not as melodic as his son's. Suspicion arose in his mind and he peeped through a chink in the window. He saw Snang-sa giving jewels to a handsome young stranger and Lhavu-dar-po playing merrily with a monkey.

At this sight, anger spurted up in his heart. He hurried down the ladder and leapt into the room, but the young man and the monkey had disappeared. Without allowing Snang-sa time for explanation, he seized her hair, beating and scolding her: "Yesterday you gave grain to a lama. Today you secretly gave jewels to a beggar. You are a prostitute who has ruined the reputation of a chieftain's family!" He kicked and cuffed Snang-sa.

Beaten by her husband and Sne-mo-ne-gtso the day before and her father-in-law today, Snang-sa was wounded all over her body. Her son Lhavu-dar-po had been led away by the chieftain and put in the care of a maid.

Snang-sa stayed alone in her room, angry, vexed and fearful, and died of her wounds that very night. Her little son, parted from his mother, could not eat or sleep. As soon as dawn came, the maid led him to Snang-sa's room to visit his mother. They saw her lying motionless on her bed. At first they thought she had fallen asleep, and called her several times without any response. When the maid touched her cold body and realized that she was not breathing, she knew that Snang-sa was dead. What a shock!

The maid hastened to report to Chieftain Grags-chen-pa and his son. Sne-mo-ne-gtso hurriedly went to the room and could not believe that Snang-sa had really died. They thought she only pretended to be dead because she had been humiliated twice. They sang together:

157

In the middle of the blue sky,

The heavenly dog seems to eat the moon;

Although the moon is partly eclipsed,

The time has not yet come.

How can the whole moon be eaten up?

Get up, Snang-sa!

In the garden a hundred flowers are in a riot of color,

Although the flowers and trees there have been in frost,

Autumn has not yet come, how can biting frost kill flowers!

Get up, Snang-sa!

In the warm, comfortable room,

Snang-sa pretends to be dead to intimidate others,

A person, after all, will fall sick,

How can a woman as young as you become dead?

Get up, Snang-sa!

Snang-sa remained silent. They looked at her closely and realized that she had really died. Father and son repented what they had done, regretting that they had beaten her so hard.

In order to expiate the sins of the dead, they offered the Buddhist service, did charitable and pious deeds and gave alms. And, on the Venerable's instructions, they placed Snang-sa's body on a wooden rack, tied it tightly with white cloth and wrapped it with *phrug* and carried it to the top of the eastern hill, preparing to cremate and bury it seven days later.

Snang-sa's soul, roaming about, came to the nether world and met the King of Hell. She said to him:

When I lived in the world,

Knowing that death lurked at the end of life,

I did not dare to cling to life;
Knowing that parting lay at the end of being together,
I did not dare to cling to warm feelings;
Knowing that poverty lay at the end of wealth,
I did not dare to cling to money;
Knowing that tolerance represents Buddha's profound intention,
I did not dare to make a lot of trouble.

The King of Hell looked in the records of birth and death and found that in Snang-sa's life there were many white pebbles and no more than one or two black pebbles, indicating that she had done no evil deeds. So he said to her:

"When I meet a good person, I lead him or her on the path of goodness. At that time, my name is Spyan-ras-gzigs (Avalokiteshvara), the God of Mercy. When meeting a bad person, I send him or her into hell; at that time my name is the God of Death. You are a good person and cannot linger here. Be quick, go back to the world!"

Returning from the nether world, Snang-sa was on top of the eastern hill. She tied the white burial cloth around her as a jacket and wrapped the *phrug* around her as a skirt. She sat cross-legged, singing:

Guardian fairy lady in the east,
With whole body pure and white as conch,
Holding a small drum in her right hand, pit-a-pat,
Taking a string of bells in her left hand, tinkling—
Gem fairy lady in the south,
Golden yellow like gold all over her body,
Holding a small drum in her right hand, pit-a-pat,
Taking a string of bells in her left hand, tinkling—
Lotus flower fairy lady in the west,

Red as agate all over her body,
Holding a small drum in her right hand, pit-a-pat,
Taking a string of bells in her left hand, tinkling—
Fairy lady of merit in the north,
Green like a kingfisher all over her body,
Holding a small drum in her right hand, pit-a-pat,
Taking a string of bells in her left hand, tinkling—
Fairy lady in the center,
Blue like indigo all over her body,
Holding a small drum in her right hand, pit-a-pat,
Taking a string of bells in her left hand, tinkling.

When the guardians of the corpse heard someone singing, they came near and saw Snang-sa sitting cross-legged, with white cloth over her body, murmuring. Terrified because they thought she was a ghost, they began picking up stones from the ground, to hit her. But she said to them, "Don't be afraid, I'm not a ghost. I've come back to life and returned to this world." They hastened to bow and greet her, and sent people to convey the news of her resurrection to her family.

Meanwhile, Snang-sa's little son Lhavu-dar-po, after his mother's death, neither drank nor ate and could not sleep at night. The maid carried him to the balcony on the roof to try to make him feel better. He asked her, "Where is my mother's graveyard? In what direction? Please tell me; it's hard for me to see her face in this life. I pray that I shall often be at her side in the next life." The maid, who had been brought by Snang-sa from her maiden home, Rgyang-vpher-knug, had been on intimate terms with her and missed her very much. The boy's words moved her and tears streamed down her cheeks. She pointed to the top of the eastern hill and told him everything.

As he gazed towards the east, Lhavu-dar-po saw several horses galloping forward to bring the message. When they heard that Snang-sa had come back to life and returned to this world, all the family felt as if they had found a piece of gold. They ran together towards the eastern hill. There they saw Snang-sa sitting at the top with a canopy of rosy clouds and a rainbow in the sky above her, and flowers raining down over her.

Chieftain Grags-chen-pa asked Snang-sa over and over to return and live with the family and run the household. He lavished praises on her virtue, intelligence and resourcefulness. He also blamed himself severely for his errors and expressed his repentance. But she was firm in her determination not to return home.

When little Lhavu-dar-po saw that his mother was unwilling to go back home, he jumped down from the maid's back and threw himself into his mother's arms, crying:

When a son is not at his mother's side,
It is like a monk away from his master,
How can he achieve enlightenment in Buddhism?
Pray think of this, mother,
Return with your son to our home village.
When a son is not at his mother's side,
It is like a citizen away from his ruler,
Nobody will give him leadership and counsel.
Pray think of this, mother,
Return with me to the home village.
When a son is not at his mother's side,
It is like an unruly horse breaking away from its reins,
However resourceful its driver is, he cannot escape death,
Pray think of this, mother,

Return with me to the home village.

When a son is not at his mother's side,

It is like a maiden unable to find a husband,

However fine her clothes and jewelry, they are of no use.

Pray think of this, mother,

Return with me to the home village.

When a son is not at his mother's side,

It is like a fine horse in its old age,

He can run, walk and compete, but he cannot win.

Pray think of this, mother,

Return with your son to the home village.

When a son is not at his mother's side,

It is like a weak mule who, however good the fodder,
  cannot be fattened.

Pray think of this, mother,

Return with your son to the home village.

When a son is not at his mother's side,

It is like a merchant in a strange place with neither
  goods nor money,

Worried and unable to show his ability.

Pray think of this, mother,

Return with your son to the home village.

When a son is not at his mother's side,

It is like an isolated column inscribed with scriptures,

No devotee has ever come to pay it homage.

Pray think of this, mother,

Return with your son to the home village.

When a son is not at his mother's side,

It is like a little bird without its wings,

Even if it flies up to the sky, it will fall down again.
Pray think of this, mother,
Return with your son to the home village.
When a son is not at his mother's side,
It is like arriving at a northern wilderness without water and grass,
Although there is an inn, nobody comes to it.
Pray think of this, mother,
Return with your son to the home village.
When a son is not at his mother's side,
It is like mange all over his body,
He is loathsome and nobody looks after him.
Pray think of this, mother,
Return with your son to the home village!

Snang-sa was moved by her son's words, but she recalled the sufferings she had undergone at home. So she said:
I am not a walking corpse,
Don't be frightened.
I am truly alive, returned from death to this world,
It's neither a dream nor a lie.
You should rejoice at this true event!
Death comes at the end of life,
How can everybody return from death to this world?
My son! I want to take up ascetic Buddhism now,
Otherwise, I will go to the King of Hell sooner or later.
Handsome lion on the snow mountain,
Don't be reluctant to part with me, little snow mountain,
The mountain range is better than I,
I am in danger of being melted by the sun;

Brave eagle flying in the sky,

Don't be reluctant to part with me, steep cliff,

King of Mount Sumeru is better than I,

I am in danger of being killed by a thunderbolt;

Beautiful double-horned David's deer,

Don't be reluctant to part with me, meadow,

Grassland with plenty of water and grass is better than I,

I am in danger of being destroyed by frost;

Golden-eyed little fish swimming as fast as wind,

Don't be reluctant to part with me, small lake on high mountain,

The vast expanse of sea is better than I,

I am in danger of being evaporated by drought;

Lark that sings melodiously on a twig,

Don't be reluctant to part with me, sparse willow woods,

A dense forest is better than I,

I am in danger of withering and losing my leaves;

Golden bee with silver wings,

Don't be reluctant to part with me, little flower of Halo,

Beautiful lotus flower is better than I,

I am in danger of being damaged by hailstones.

Delicate good little son Lhavu-dar-po,

Don't be reluctant to part with mother Snang-sa,

The chieftain and his son are better than I,

I am unwilling to return to our home village.

Although his mother had poured out her heart, Lhavu-dar-po still
cried and pleaded with her to return home. He said:

Little lion on the snow mountain,

Reluctant to part with snow mountain;

164

Even if he is not damaged by rain or snow,

It is impossible for beautiful mane to grow on his body.

Before little lion's mane has fully grown,

Pray snow mountain, remain for the time being.

After little lion's mane has fully grown,

He will make a pilgrimage to worship Buddha together with snow
   mountain.

To prevent the sun from melting snow mountain,

Little lion may ask black shadow to shield it.

Little eagle on a precipitous cliff,

Reluctant to part with precipitous cliff;

Even if he shuns the hunter's rifle and arrow,

No feather will grow on his wings.

Wait until feathers have grown on little eagle's wings,

He will make a pilgrimage to worship Buddha together with
   precipitous cliff.

To prevent thunderbolt from hitting at precipitous cliff,

Little eagle may invite the Venerable with supernatural power to
   avert disaster by prayer.

Little deer on a meadow,

Reluctant to part with the meadow;

Even if he may not be wounded by the bite of a hound,

No pretty antler will grow on his head.

Before antlers have grown on its head,

Pray meadow, remain for now.

Wait until antlers have grown on his head,

It will make pilgrimage to worship Buddha together with the
   meadow.

To prevent the meadow from being hit by frost,

Little deer may invite rosy clouds from the south.

Golden-eyed little fish in a lake,

Reluctant to part with the lake;

Even if it may not be caught by a hook,

It cannot learn the art of dodging, whirling and turning.

Before little fish has learned dodging, whirling and turning,

Pray lake water, remain for now.

Wait until little fish has learned dodging, whirling and turning,

It will make pilgrimage to worship Buddha together with lake
  water.

To prevent the drought demon from drying up the lake,

Little fish may invite the dragon king and queen to come and help.

A lark in the willow woods,

Reluctant to part with the willow woods;

Even if it may not be injured or killed by falcons,

It will never learn the art of singing.

Before it has learned the art of singing,

Pray willow woods, remain for now.

Wait until the lark has learned the art of singing,

It may make a pilgrimage to worship Buddha
  together with willow woods.

To prevent the twigs and leaves of willow woods from withering,

Little lark may ask the God of Summer to stay here long.

Little golden bee in the midst of Halo flower,

Reluctant to part with Halo flower;

Even if it may not be injured by the pecking of birds,

No silver wings will grow on its body.

Before silver wings have grown on little golden bee's body,

Pray Halo flower, remain for now.

Wait until silver wings have grown on little golden bee's body,
It will make a pilgrimage to worship Buddha
   together with Halo flower.
To prevent hailstones from damaging Halo flower,
Little golden bee may invite you to decorate the vase.
Little son Lhavu-dar-po,
Reluctant to part with mother Snang-sa;
Even if he may not die and see the God of Hell at once,
He cannot grow strong and robust.
Before little son has grown strong and robust,
Mama, pray return with us to the home village;
Wait until little son grows strong and robust,
He will make a pilgrimage to worship Buddha together with his
   mama.
To help his mother avoid persecution,
Little son can do whatever is within his ability to do.

The chieftain and his son and all the men, women and servants entreated Snang-sa to return home. She pitied her son and also wanted to go home, thinking she would seize this chance to persuade people to convert to Buddhism and encourage them to do pious, charitable deeds. So she consented to their entreaties and returned home with them.

In the course of time, the chieftain and his son gradually ignored her teaching and did not even allow her to believe in Buddhist preachings. Therefore, she took her son to her parents' home in Rgyang-vpher-knug for a visit. On the way, she expounded Buddhist preachings to the other passengers and the boatman, all of whom praised her for it. When she arrived, she greeted her parents and told them all the sufferings she had undergone. They were overjoyed at her return, but they grieved when they heard the sufferings she had experienced.

In her home village Snang-sa also met the girl companions of her youth and stroked the loom where she used to weave cloth. Her heart was full as she realized that years were fleet-footed and life was short. So she resolved to become a nun and dedicate her life to ascetic Buddhism.

Late one quiet, moonlit night, Snang-sa went to seek refuge in Skyid-po-yar-klung Monastery, asking Sha-kya-rgyal-mtshan lama to accept her as a nun. The lama devised ways to test her devotion. When he saw that she was truly devoted to Buddhism, he accepted her as a nun and taught her the rites, scriptures and ways of quiet meditation.

When Chieftain Grags-chen-pa and his son heard that Snang-sa had gone to a monastery and become a nun without their permission, they were very angry and assembled all the common folk between 16 and 18 years old who were under their jurisdiction. With guns and swords in their hands, they encircled Skyid-po-yar-klung Monastery to arrest Sha-kya-rgyal-mtshan lama and Snang-sa-vod-vbum. But the lama, showing his supernatural power, flew into the sky and only then were the chieftain and his son convinced.

Later, Chieftain Grags-chen-pa and his son came to believe in Buddhism. At that time, they not only allowed Snang-sa to become a nun but gave administrative and household authority to the son, Lhavu-dar-po. They even became monks, underwent ascetic Buddhist training and achieved enlightenment. Snang-sa-vod-vbum flew up to heaven. Her footprints were left as if engraved in the mountain cave where she had practiced Buddhist teachings.

Lhavu-dar-po performed ten pious, charitable deeds and abandoned ten evil deeds during the time he was administrator. Rich harvests were gathered in the locality every year and everybody led a peaceful, happy life.

PAD-MA-VOD-VBAR

This opera was written at Saskya in south central Tibet in the summer of 1960, following an oral account of the legend. The narrator was Bkro-shi don-grub, a veteran actor of the Tibetan opera. He was both director and actor of the Saskya Theatrical Troupe. He dictated the entire opera in three days, which largely maintains the plot, order and singing as it was performed on the stage. Therefore, it may be read as a story or performed as an opera.

The leading character of the opera, Pad-ma-vod-vbar, is regarded as an image of Great Master Pad-ma-cbyung-gnas. A high monk of Kri-srong Ideb-tsan, Tibetan king in the 8th century, Great Master Pad-ma-vbyung-gnas preached the doctrine of the old school of Buddhism. He and the king and Great Master Zhi-wa-vtsho are known as "the three virtuous men in Tibet." Today various parts of Tibet have relics of stories about Great Master Pad-ma-vbyung-gnas conquering monsters and demons. There is also a book "Teachings Left by Pad-ma" specializing in his stories. Because he was the first hero who appeared in Tibetan dances portraying the subduing of demons and monsters to influence people, some persons say he was the founder of silent drama—the origin of Tibetan opera.

Once upon a time, there was a king named Mu-stegs Rgyal-po, meaning "the king of pearls." He had a minister nicknamed "the Crippled Minister." There was also a wealthy merchant called

Nor-bzang. The king did not trust the merchant, fearing Nor-bzang
would seize his throne someday. So he planned to remove the
merchant. One day he said to the minister:

Crippled Minister, son of the postal officer,
There where the sun rises,
Is Sgrol-ma Lha-khang, a jolly manor.
A merchant named Nor-bzang and his wife,
Fairy Dung-can-ma, live there.
You go quickly there,
And for me summon Nor-bzang the trader.
Just go without delay,
And on the way don't kill the hour.

Holding up the front of his long gown, the Crippled Minister said:
I'm going to Sgrol-ma Lha-khang
As you order.

Arriving in the manor, he shouted in an arbitrary voice:
Merchant Nor-bzang, listen to our king's order.
You must go to him promptly,
Leaving the Sgrol-ma Lha-khang manor.

The merchant did not dare to delay. He hurried to the palace and
kowtowed to the king. The king said:

Very good! You must have suffered,
Coming a long way in a hurry.
You've purchased and shipped goods for me everywhere;
From Mngav-ris to near and far Tibet,
Then from other places to Ali in the same manner.

171

From the south you transported things to Jiangtang in the north,
Then on to the other bank across the Yarlung Zangbo River.
You've been busy buying silks and satins for my ministers,
As well as precious things I treasure.
Many learn of your merits;
Who doesn't praise you with pleasure?
But my treasure house is still short of one thing.
It is Dgos-vdod-vbum-vbyor,* a priceless treasure.
Go to sea as soon as possible,
And fetch me this treasure.

The merchant was startled at the king's order. He replied:
Oh! King Mu-stegs, please listen to me instead.
I've purchased goods for you,
Busy going north and south and everywhere.
It's my duty to pledge loyalty to Your Majesty.
Now I'm weak as I grow older.
I'm not able to go to sea.
There are many capable men in the state here and there.
Why send an old man to his grave?

The king was very angry. He thundered:
Shut up and don't bluster!
If you're unwilling to go to sea,
I'll punish you according to law and order.
And your wife will become a prisoner.

---

* See the opera "Prince Dri-med-leun-idan."

The merchant was frightened and did not dare offend the king. He said:

All right, when necessary things are prepared,

I'll certainly sail out to sea.

First, I need an enormous ship with a horse-head bow in the harbor.*

Second, we need a hundred loads of tiger-head trees.**

Third, a hundred loads of ox-head trees must be brought there.***

Fourth, I want the Parrot of Foresight.

Fifth, there must be a harbinger of dawn, a red rooster.

Sixth, we need she-goats that lead the way.

Seventh, I want five hundred assistants all together.

I'll put to sea when the seven things are ready.

The king gathered all the carpenters, blacksmiths and other skillful craftsmen in the kingdom and collected all the necessary materials. One by one, he prepared all the things Nor-bzang needed. The merchant had to do nothing but go to sea. Sailing the horse-head ship, the crew and the merchant arrived at the gate of the palace of the sea dragons. Two dragons, one black and the other white, came out of the gate and upset the ship, drowning all on board.

When he heard of the merchant's death at sea, King Mu-stegs was full of joy. He thought his throne would be safe and secure from then on.

When the merchant had set sail, his wife was pregnant. After his

---

* All Tibetan boats have a horse-head bow, as dragon boats have a dragon head at the front.

** The Tibetan tiger-head tree has hard wood with fine grain.

*** The Tibetan ox-head tree produces light wood.

death, she gave birth to a son named Pad-ma-vod-vbar. She thought: "The king has murdered my husband. If he knows I have a son, my child will have to die." Therefore, she kept and raised the baby in a secret room. The boy grew up. One day he asked:

Fairy Dung-can-ma, my mother,

Who is my father?

Which family does my mother belong to as a member?

Why is there a child without a father?

After thinking for a while, the mother answered:

I don't know who is your father.

Don't make random guesses.

Neither am I your own mother.

I adopted you as the son of a beggar.

The son didn't believe his mother. One day he went into the hills to collect firewood. When he returned in the evening, he said:

I saw a herd of deer on the grassland there.

The buck led in front,

While the doe who is the mother followed behind.

The fawns trotted in the middle.

Even wild animals are blessed with a family life somewhere.

Why can't I see my father?

The mother said nothing as before. Some days later, the son went outdoors and played with the other children living nearby. In any game they played, Pad-ma-vod-vbar would win without exception. The other children grew angry and made fun of him, saying:

The father was like a sandalwood tree,

While the son is a tiny blade of hay!
That boy is the first to win
Whatever game we play.

This added to Pad-ma-vod-vbar's sorrow. He ran home and pestered his mother for an answer:

Mama Fairy Dung-can-ma,
Please tell me the truth today.
All the other boys shouted at me
When I went outdoors to play:
"The father was like a sandalwood tree,
While the son is a tiny blade of hay!"
Tell me who is the sandalwood tree?
And who is the tiny blade of hay?
If you tell me Father's story in detail,
I pledge myself to continue his cause some day.

His mother was pleased to hear this, but she dared not tell him the story. Many days passed by. One day a festive fair took place at Lhar-phyin. Pad-ma-vod-vbar took eighteen strands of coarse-color yarn and nineteen strands of fine-color yarn and went to the fair.

There was a very old woman named Dpen-tshig-ma at the fair. No one was older than she. She was 180 years old. She was selling shells at a stall. Pad-ma-vod-vbar came before her stall and said, "Old Granny, do you want to barter things with me?" The old lady replied:

Little darling, let's go into the sandalwood forest
To barter our things.
Because persons here like to make all sorts of comments,
And there are too many people and their loose tongues.

175

The two went into the forest and felt each other's fingers in their long sleeves.* After feeling and counting fingers for a long while, the boy took away all the old lady's shells and gave her only a little strand of yarn. Getting into a huff, she said:

The father was like a sandalwood tree,

While the son is a tiny blade of hay.

I've accumulated all these shells in my life,

In a single morning you, swindler, take them away.

The boy eagerly asked the old lady:

Old Granny, don't be angry,

I only play a trick on you.

If you tell me my father's story,

I'll never forget your kindness.

Here are eighteen strands of yarn ready

   to reward you for your goodness.

If you tell me my mother's history,

neither will I forget your kindness.

Here are nineteen strands of colored yarn ready

   to reward you for your goodness.

And all your shells come in handy;

I'll return them to you and you'll be happy.

The old lady was glad. She caressed the boy's head and said:

Pad-ma-vod-vbar, listen carefully.

---

* It is a custom for the Tibetans to do business by feeling and counting each other's fingers in their sleeves. The number of fingers signifies figures and the price of goods.

Your father was a man whose praises people sang.

Shipping goods north and south,

He was a merchant named Nor-bzang.

King Mu-stegs sent him out to sea,

And he never returned, alive or dead, with his crew.

Fairy Dung-can-ma is your mother.

She's still living in Sgrol-ma Lha-khang.

Hearing this, the boy was pleased. He gave the old lady all his fine and coarse yarns and the shells. He went home, singing all the way. His mother was surprised at seeing him in such high spirits. The son said to the mother:

I've been to the fair,

And heard the sweetest words there.

It's the finest weather ever,

Now I know who is my father.

He was Nor-bzang the trader,

Who was sent out to sea by the king and returned never.

You're my own mother.

Why do you to this day keep the truth from me?

This worried the mother, who hastily said:

Nor-bzang the Merchant was your father.

The king sent him out to sea, plotting his murder.

He has never returned, alive or dead, from far away.

The sorrow always weighs on my mind.

The king will not let you go,

If he knows you're the son of your father.

And we, mother and son, will suffer disaster.

Go quickly and hide yourself in your room.

I'm able to manage our household matters.

Allowing no argument, she shut her son in the room and refused to let him out again.

One day King Mu-stegs visited the market fair and sauntered about here and there. Looking at this and that, he praised it:

This is a fair large and wide with a big crowd.

Here rich merchants sell gold and silver.

Middle merchants are silk and satin traders.

Small merchants display piece goods before customers.

Ah! What's in the hands of the old lady,

Brighter than the sun and moon,

Fresh and gorgeous and dazzling like a flower.

It is splendid yarns, and who's the spinner?

Ministers, go quickly and find out the maker.

The Crippled Minister unsheathed his glittering sword and went limping to the old lady Dpen-tshig-ma. He shouted at her:

Old woman Dpen-tshig-ma, listen.

Where did you gather these splendid yarns?

Who has spun the yarns and twisted the threads?

She lives in which county, which village, which manor?

The old lady was frightened and trembled. Shuddering at the minister's sword, she replied:

You've come in time, Crippled Minister.

You've covered a tiresome trip far from the palace.

These splendid yarns in my hands,

Were produced by me, the spinner.

They came not from another county.

Nor were they from another village bartered.

The Crippled Minister didn't believe her. He yelled at her to give her a jolt. Seizing her white hair, he threatened: "If you, old fox, refuse to speak the truth, I'll strike with my sword and send you to your old home!" Scared out of her wits, the old lady spoke the truth:

Your Excellency, Your Excellency,

Please spare the life of this old-timer.

I'm going to tell you the truth.

But don't go and harm others.

Pad-ma-vod-vbar sold me these yarns.

He's the son of Nor-bzang the Trader.

The young man is able and clever.

Sgrol-ma Lha-khang is where he makes his home.

Letting go of the old lady, the Crippled Minister went to the king and reported:

King Mu-stegs, listen to my report.

I've toured the fair.

I daren't look at this or that.

I daren't loiter here and there.

I've found out who's the spinner.

For Your Majesty it's an essential matter.

It was Pad-ma-vod-vbar, son of the trader,

Who sold the yarns to the old-timer.

He is a boy able and clever.

Sgrot-ma Lha-khang is where he makes his home.

The king was alarmed at the news that Nor-bzang had a son. He hurriedly gave orders:

Crippled Minister, listen to me carefully.

Over Sgrol-ma Lha-khang rosy clouds have hovered,

And magnificent golden rays have shimmered;

Because Pad-ma-vod-vbar was born there.

No wonder my mind had misgivings.

Nor-bzang has a successor.

Crippled Minister, go quickly,

And bring the boy hither.

The minister went to Sgro-ma Lha-khang as ordered. He kicked up a row, shouting:

Dung-can-ma, you daredevil,

After bearing an able son, why didn't you come to register?

Now the king demands his presence,

According to a royal order.

Dung-can-ma was frightened and trembled all over. "What do you say?" she said. "Nor-bzang has been wandering many years far away. I've seen no shadow of him. How can there be a son without a father? Minister, please show kindness and mercy!"

The minister turned a deaf ear to her. His face was ablaze with anger. He yelled:

You devil of a woman,

Refuse to behave well.

I'm going to teach you a lesson,

Sending you to the King of Hell!

He rushed forward to attack Dung-can-ma. At this juncture, Pad-ma-vod-vbar, who was hiding in his room, could contain himself no longer. He leapt out of his room and said:

Crippled Minister, don't commit violence.

Pad-ma-vod-vbar fears no death or murder.

I commit myself to my own business.

Why do harm to my mother?

The Crippled Minister seized the boy, tied his hands and took him to the palace. Seeing the young man, the king ordered him to be untied, saying hypocritically:

So you've come, very good, Pad-ma-vod-vbar.

I've heard of you a short time ago.

I see you are proud and clever.

Compared with Prince Gesar,*

Your ability and skill in martial arts are greater.

Since ancient times,

Sons have carried on the undertakings of their fathers,

And paid the debts owed by their ancestors.

Now you must go out to sea and seek my treasure.

I'll take care of your family matters.

If you bring back Dgos-vdod-vbum-vbyor, the treasure,

Upon you, young man, a great merit I'll confer.

Pad-ma-vod-vbar knew what the king wanted to do. Without caring

---

* Prince Gesar is a hero in Tibetan legend. There is a Tibetan epic entitled *The Story of Prince Gesar*.

much, he replied:

King Mu-stegs, please sit at rest and listen to me.

I'll put out to sea abiding by your order.

You must order various things to be prepared,

Because it's an extraordinary event to sail the distant ocean.

First, I want the precious luck-bringing *ruyi*.

Second, I need five hundred workers.

Third, there must be dairy cows.

Fourth, there must be a good amount of fodder.

Fifth, I want an elephant that is steady as a mountain.

Sixth, I need horses fast as the whirlwind, not slower.

Seventh, I want a parrot that is able to see the future.

Eighth, I need food enough for the journey we cover.

As soon as these are all prepared,

I'll navigate the distant seas.

Seeing that the young man had fallen into his trap, the king was pleased. Nodding his head, he promised all these things, saying:

All right, very well.

I'll prepare all these hither.

You may have a seven-day leave to stay with your mother.

You must set sail seven days from now.

Returning home, Pad-ma-vod-vbar told his mother all about the king's order. This worried her, and she said:

Hearing that my little darling has to go to sea,

I'm afraid we'll never meet again, son and mother.

Another man sailed the seas earlier.

There is no news of him, who must be dead; it's your father.

Cruel King Mu-stegs now deceives you.

Is it easy to explore the seas for the treasure?

Overwhelmed with grief, she went to the Prince Gesar Pagoda and prayed to God for blessing. A fairy flew down from the East Peak and said to her:

Pad-ma-vod-vbar sets sail but will return home.

Namobuddhaya Namogurudakiya is a secret incantation

    that works wonders.

Keep it in your mind,

And no harm you'll ever suffer.

Returning home, she told her son about the fairy and the secret incantation and urged him to learn it by heart. Seven days passed by quickly. Pad-ma-vod-vbar reported to the king. He and his 500 assistants put out to sea.

As they neared the gate of the dragon palace, they saw two dragons, one black and the other white, coming to meet them and to upset their ship. At this juncture, the prophetic parrot spoke:

Pad-ma-vod-vbar, Pad-ma-vod-vbar,

The gate of the dragon palace is a little farther.

Two dragons, one black and one white,

Are coming to upset our boat.

Chant the incantation and don't linger.

Pad-ma-vod-vbar prayed, muttering:

Mother has told me that

The flying fairy related to her the wondrous incantation.

Now please show your magic power,

And make the waters calmer.

Indeed, the two dragons disappeared and the sea became calm and quiet. Safely the ship passed through the gate of the dragon palace and came to an island, Pad-ma-vod-vbar put his 500 assistants on the island along with the dairy cows, horses, food, fodder and the elephant. He himself went alone to the bottom of the sea to fetch the treasure from the dragon palace. In the dragon palace, a mother-of-pearl princess kept the treasure Dgos-vdod-vbum-vbyor. Seeing the young man come alone into the palace, she admired him and said, "You'd better stay in our palace forever. If you're not willing, then stay three years, or at least three months."

The young man replied:

In the magnificent dragon palace I can't linger,
Because there's King Mu-stegs' urgent order.
If I stay three years hither,
Who at home will attend to my mother?
And on the island there are five hundred workers.
Who will take care of them there?
I can stay only three days hither,
And delay no longer.

Therefore, Pad-ma-vod-vbar, who was actually Buddha's incarnation as human being, stayed in the dragon palace for three days. He bestowed grace upon everyone in the palace. As a result, all who were blind could see again and deaf-mutes recovered their hearing and power of speech. Handicapped persons were restored to good health. The children of the dragons thanked and respected Pad-ma-vod-vbar. They presented the treasure Dgos-vdod-vbum-vbyor to him. Carrying the treasure, the young man went back to the island. His 500 assistants had waited three years for him, because three days in the dragon palace were equal to three years in the human world. Pad-ma-vod-vbar said:

Your son has come home;
My five hundred good workers,
For three years you've waited hither.
Now I'm going ahead home as a harbinger.
You sail slowly till we meet together.

With the help of the magic treasure, Pad-ma-vod-vbar reached home in a blink of the eye. His mother had had no news of him for three years. She had grieved and fallen ill, and was bed-ridden. Pad-ma-vod-vbar knocked at the door, saying:

Your son has come home;
Open the door, Mother.
No words can exhaust my experience.
Let me tell it from the beginning, later.

Lying in bed, the mother feebly replied:
Who's knocking hard at the door?
Why come to bully an old woman going to her doom?
My son has gone to sea.
How can he return home?

With anxiety, Pad-ma-vod-vbar shouted:
It's me Pad-ma-vod-vbar, and no other!
Your son has come home without destruction.
Open the door, Mother!
Let me tell you my heartfelt emotion.

185

Muttering to herself, the mother struggled out of bed and opened the door. It really was Pad-ma-vod-vbar! The mother had grown decrepit in three years. The son put Dgos-vdod-vbum-vbyor on her head and prayed aloud:

Mother has said,

The flying fairy granted us a wondrous incantation.

If the treasure has magic power,

Let my mother recover her youth and vigor!

All of a sudden, his mother was restored to her former appearance. Wrinkles in her face were no more. Her white hair turned black again. Mother and son were overjoyed.

Later, Pad-ma-vod-vbar's 500 assistants returned. The young man and his mother treated the entire crew to festive celebrations for days.

Meanwhile, King Mu-stegs was harboring all sorts of suspicions. He said to the Crippled Minister:

Why does the din of rejoicing rise to the sky,

Over Sgrol-ma Lha-khang there?

Why above the area,

Does bright light flicker?

Why do the walls of the manor,

Shine with oil and shimmer?

Is Pad-ma-vod-vbar back home there?

Go quickly and bring him hither.

The Crippled Minister went to Sgrol-ma Lha-khang and brought Pad-ma-vod-vbar to the king. The king was surprised, afraid and ruffled. He said:

Pad-ma-vod-vbar, thank you,

For the hardships you have suffered.
Have you brought back Dgos-vdod-vbum-vbyor the treasure?
It's something I can't forget.

Pad-ma-vod-vbar said:
Your Majesty, let me report to you.
I've sailed the distant seas.
We didn't make our journey in vain.
We've brought back Dgos-vdod-vbum-vbyor the treasure.
Now let me present Your Majesty,
The treasure along with its favor.

The king told the young man to go home to have a good rest. Nevertheless, something weighed heavy on his mind. He hit upon another evil idea. He planned to send Pad-ma-vod-vbar to the state of Raksasa* to fetch other treasures, so that the young man would perish there. He summoned Pad-ma-vod-vbar again and said:
Go west to the state of Raksasa.
From there you fetch a gold pot and a silver spoon,
    both treasures.
If you can bring back Dgos-vdod-vbum-vbyor,
You surely can get these treasures.

Pad-ma-vod-vbar couldn't turn down the king's order, so he promised to go. He set out for the state of Raksasa alone. He came to the pass overlooking the state. It was a fort cast with liquid iron. The

_____

* The story goes that Raksasa was a land of man-eating monsters somewhere to the west.

187

raksasa defending the pass roared:

Hey, it's queer!

There's no human being here,

But why smell I the flesh of man?

I've not tasted warm human meat for three years altogether.

I've not drunk warm human blood either.

Come on, come out quicker.

I'll eat your meat and drink your blood,

Then I'll live much longer.

The raksasa searched the place and caught Pad-ma-vod-vbar. He seized and swallowed the young man at one gulp. Once inside the raksasa's stomach. Pad-ma-vod-vbar chanted:

Mother has told me,

That the flying fairy's incantation works wonders.

Let me go out of raksasa's stomach,

If the incantation really has magic power.

Namobuddhaya Namogurudakiya!

Namobuddhaya Namogurudakiya!

The raksasa began to vomit. He was so pained that he rolled on the ground. Finally he threw up the young man from his stomach and said:

Alas! Alas!

I didn't know you're none other than Buddha himself.

I vow to repent of my behavior.

Evil-doings have gone on forever.

But from now on I'll not perform them further.

For the night I'm preparing your quarters.

Tomorrow I'll show you the way farther.

I've horse and donkey meat for your dinner,[*]
There's nothing better!

So Pad-ma-vod-vbar stayed overnight at the pass. The next morning he continued to go west and arrived at the residence of the queen of the state of Raksasa. The queen sensed something unusual and cried:

Hey, it's queer!
There's no human being here,
But why smell I the flesh of man?
I've not tasted warm human meat for three years altogether.
I've not drunk warm human blood either.
Come on, come out quicker.
I'll eat your meat and drink your blood,
Then I'll live much longer.

She searched all corners and found Pad-ma-vod-vbar. She exclaimed:

A Tibetan comes to the secluded kingdom of Raksasa—
It's not an ordinary matter.
You've passed one test but not another.
Today is an auspicious date in the calendar.

She swallowed the young man at one gulp. Once in her stomach, Pad-ma-vod-vbar chanted the incantation. The raksasa queen was in great pain and began to vomit. Groaning and panting, she said:

I didn't know that you're divine.

---

[*] Tibetans are not used to eating horse or donkey meat.

189

Nor did I know you're Buddha and no other.
Do you want to come out through my mouth?
Or to pass through my other end?

From her stomach Pad-ma-vod-vbar replied:
If you don't want your intestines to be destroyed,
Let me quickly come out through your mouth.
I'm Buddha's incarnation;
How can I go through your other end?

Growing nervous, the raksasa queen promised to give Pad-ma-vod-vbar the two treasures of a gold pot and a silver spoon and asked him to come out rapidly. She said:
I'm the mother of sixty-eight children.
Please forgive me, an ignorant woman.
I'll give you my family heirloom, a silver spoon and a gold pot.
Please come out quickly so that my nerves can be quietened.

Pad-ma-vod-vbar came out of the queen's mouth. Receiving the treasures, he sat in the gold pot and knocked it with the silver spoon. The gold pot flew into the sky, carrying the young man home to his mother. They had a merry get-together.
King Mu-stegs said to the Crippled Minister:
Look at Sgrol-ma Lha-khang over there.
It's bright and glittering like a fairyland manor.
In the sky rosy clouds and mist hover.
The sound of drums and gongs grows louder and louder.
I'm afraid that boy is back home yonder.
He makes me nervous day and night.

Go there and find out about the matter.
If he's back, bring him hither.

The Crippled Minister went to Sgrol-ma Lha-khang and brought
Pad-ma-vod-vbar before the king. The king said:
You daredevil, Pad-ma-vod-vbar,
Why hide at home and not carry out my order with pleasure?
Have you been to the state of Raksasa?
Have you brought back the two treasures?

Pad-ma-vod-vbar unhurriedly presented the gold pot and silver
spoon to the king. He said:
King Mu-stegs, listen to me.
I've gone west as you ordered.
Arriving in the state of Raksasa,
I've brought back extraordinary treasures.
They can fly you into the sky
And take you to places to the east, west, north or south, anywhere.
You can watch everything underneath you,
And admire the scenery the world over.

The king itched for a ride in the gold pot. Asking Pad-ma-vod-vbar
to escort him, he sat in the pot with the young man. Pad-ma-vod-vbar
knocked the gold pot with the silver spoon. The gold pot rose into the
sky and flew west to the state of Raksasa. Arriving over the pass that
was cast of liquid iron, the king laughed and said:
Aha! It's an interesting place.
The peak is cast with liquid iron,
As is the land around it.

Iron fluid flows in the river.

The fort is built of iron.

It's really a wonder.

But alas!

My head suffers a great pain.

I feel like vomiting.

Let Buddha in heaven hear my prayers,

And protect me so that I return home safe and sound.

Pad-ma-vod-vbar, my good brother,

Let's touch down quickly on solid ground.

Pad-ma-vod-vbar replied, "It's still early. We're going to a more interesting place of hustle and bustle." In a moment, they were over the palace of the queen of the state of Raksasa. Pad-ma-vod-vbar shouted: "Come! All of you sixty-eight raksasa. Come on! Eat your refreshments!" He threw King Mu-stegs down from the gold pot. The king fell dead on the ground and was eaten up by the raksasa.

Pad-ma-vod-vbar rode the gold pot back to the king's palace and took over the throne. Since then the entire nation has enjoyed a happy life.

Eulogy

Dear audience, please listen to my explanation.

Under favorable auspices of Buddha thereafter,

Enjoying the sixty-three good omens and good luck in body,

    mouth and intention,*

---

* "Body, mouth and intention" mean entire body and soul to Buddhists.

The previous life of Great Master Pad-ma-vbyung-gnas[*]
    was born an orphan without father.
On the coast of an immense ocean,
He appeared from the stamen of the wonderful lotus flower.
We wish him always to stay away from the
    suffering of transmigration.
We wish him to be living in this world forever.

---

   * Great Master Pad-ma-vbyung-gnas was the founder of the old school of
Lamaism. The legend says he is Pad-ma-vod-vbar's life in the next incarnation.

图书在版编目（CIP）数据

藏剧故事选：英文 / 王尧主编 . -- 北京：新世界
出版社，2013.3
ISBN 978-7-5104-4104-2

Ⅰ．①藏… Ⅱ．①王… Ⅲ．①藏族－民间故事－作品
集－中国－英文 Ⅳ．① I277.3

中国版本图书馆 CIP 数据核字（2013）第 044077 号

Tales from Tibetan Opera
藏剧故事选

作　　者：王　尧
翻　　译：王　尧
责任编辑：李淑娟　闫传海
英文审校：Paul Adams
装帧设计：贺玉婷
版式设计：清鑫工作室
责任印制：李一鸣　黄厚清
出版发行：北京　新世界出版社
社　　址：北京市西城区百万庄大街24号（100037）
总编室电话：＋86 10 6899 5424　　68326679（传真）
发行部电话：＋86 10 6899 5968　　68998705（传真）
本社中文网址：http://www.nwp.cn
版权部电子信箱：frank@nwp.com.cn
版权部电话：＋86 10 6899 6306
印　　刷：北京京华虎彩印刷有限公司
经　　销：新华书店
开　　本：787×1290　　1/16
字　　数：100千字　　印张：12.75
版　　次：2013年4月第1版　　2013年4月北京第1次印刷
书　　号：ISBN 978-7-5104-4104-2
定　　价：56.00元